THE DANCE *of the*
BUSINESS MIND

**Book inspired by the now 7-time
#1 *World Professional Latin Dance Champion,*
Riccardo Cocchi**

THE DANCE *of the* BUSINESS MIND

Strategies to Thrive Anywhere, From the Ballroom to the Boardroom

VALEH NAZEMOFF

Bestselling author of *The Four Intelligences of the Business Mind*

TI Press

The Dance of the Business Mind:
Strategies to Thrive Anywhere, From the Ballroom to the Boardroom

This book is available at a discount when purchased in quantity for sales promotions or corporate use. Special editions, which include personalized covers, excerpts, and corporate imprints can be created when purchased in large quantities. For more information, please email media@acolyst.com or call 844.226.5978 ext. 106, or visit www.valehnazemoff.com.

First Edition
Paperback ISBN-13: 978-0-9987794-0-9
Kindle ISBN-13: 978-0-9987794-1-6
Library of Congress Control Number: 2017903360

I dedicate this book to you, the reader, as you invite your mind to dance its way through life's key moments of decision making. Make your mind dance while connecting with your body and soul. Transformation requires the action, movement, and motion of dance in order to drive change and deliver results. Be passionate about your purpose and let the power of your dancing mind lead you forward to illuminate the world!

To Make Better Decisions,
Free Your Mind to Dance!

– Valeh Nazemoff

Opportunity dances with those
who are already on the dance floor.

– H. Jackson Brown Jr.

CONTENTS

Great dancers are not great because of their technique,
they are great because of their passion

– MARTHA GRAHAM

You must give everything to make your life as beautiful
as the dreams that dance in your imagination.

– ROMAN PAYNE

ACKNOWLEDGMENTS

The inspiration for this book and its resulting journey was driven by fate and brought together by a collection of amazingly brilliant energy. This book was brought to life thanks to the monumental contributions of many great and wonderful people.

To the man who inspired this book, Riccardo Cocchi, I am forever grateful!

To Genya Bartashevich, my dance partner and coach, thank you for working with me, sometimes till late hours brainstorming, reviewing, editing, re-editing, and, most importantly, dancing. To Yana Mazhnikova, my friend and coach, thank you for sharing your stories and helping me connect with the emotional side at the core of the partnership of dance.

I am indebted to the many dance champions and adjudicators who contributed through private lessons, workshops, or late night phone calls. Thank you Vibeke Toft, Allan Tornsberg, Edita Daniute, Mirko Gozzoli, Ina Jeliazkova, Troels Bager, Polina Pilipenchuk, Dasha Sushko, Karina Smirnoff, and Slavik Kryklyvyy.

To Lydia Petrigova and Laura Alina Alexandru, thank you for your enthusiasm and love, creating opportunities for me to gather needed information for my book and this journey.

To the dance organizers who put on great events so spectators like me can learn and continue to be inspired, thank you!

It's impossible to adequately thank everyone who supported me on this journey. Shawn Rene Zimmerman, thank you for your sparkling, infectious positive energy and spirit. Beth Kaplan, heartfelt gratitude for sharing your respected advice on the correlation between balance in the boardroom and the ballroom. Arianna Huffington, I adore and admire you. Thank you for giving my voice a platform on *The Huffington Post*.

Writing this book has made me acutely aware (again) of how incredibly fortunate I am to be surrounded with such a supportive, loving, caring, determined, passionate, goal-oriented, focused crew.

Tracy Grigoriades, a million (make that a billion) thanks for being with me (again) every step of the way on this project. You have kept it light, fun, and sane, as best you could. You are still the most talented, detailed, efficient, collaborative, and remarkable professional and friend. Thank you for your enthusiasm in your support (yes, emotionally too!) to bring this message to the world.

To Mahesh Grossman, whose herculean efforts, deep insights, and incredible support were invaluable. Thank you for the long nights spent converting my written thoughts and numerous interviews into a manageable manuscript.

Thank you, Steve Bennett, and the AuthorBytes team – throughout the process of working on this project, you remained steady, present, helpful, attentive, and punctual in pushing to meet the deadlines set. Thank you for sharing a great amount of enthusiasm for this project. It is always fun brainstorming with you to translate ideas into presentable art.

Marissa Eigenbrood, Mallory Campoli, Mike Onorato, and Sandra Poirier Smith, my publicity team, who believe, as enthusiastically as I, that this book can impact society; a heartfelt gratitude.

Steve Harrison and the Quantum Leap team, thank you for helping me identify when and how to voice my message. Your marketing guidance and encouragement has helped me spread my message far and wide.

Special thanks also go to the many other all-stars that continuously support me throughout the days; my legal, bookkeeping, accounting, marketing, and other overhead team members.

Thank you, Cary Bayer, my breakthrough coach, with whom I first shared the idea of this book. He is the one who said it was fate and encouraged me to do it. I am so glad I listened to you and the voice deep down inside me.

Thank you to my champions and supporters in the partner community and colleagues at *CRN Magazine* (The Channel Company); Jennifer Follett and Gina Narcisi.

To my clients, business partners, sponsors, colleagues past and present, thank you for being the drive and motivation to share my story, pushing me to be the best version of myself, and directly influencing my thought process and achievements.

Thank you to the works of my mentor, Mark Waldman, who brilliantly and generously brings awareness to the way we communicate through neuroscience; and to others like Jim Kwik and Jason Silva, who educate our society about the magnificent capabilities of our minds.

Special thanks to Tony Robbins and Lewis Howes for bringing a different level of energy and insight, and for being role models of vision, purpose, passion, and greatness that the world so desperately needs.

There are many movers and shakers who inspire and impact society by being business leaders, dancers or entrepreneurs that need to be acknowledged for their impact on this "dancing mind" revolutionary movement – Jennifer Lopez, the judges and professionals of *Dancing with the Stars*, Shakira, Marie Forleo and the many others who enlighten the world with their insight and wisdom.

On a personal level, this movement started, unbeknownst to me, when I watched *Dancing with the Stars'* Tony Dovolani performing the Mambo live in Florida, with his then pro partner Elena Grinenko, to Shakira's "Hips Don't Lie." I didn't realize a man could shake like that. He told me after his performance that I could sign up for lessons with him. I thank him for opening me up to the world of ballroom partnership dancing.

When I returned home after my trip, I was encouraged to take on Latin partner style dancing. Two of my male friends jumped in and supported the beginning of my journey. Looking back, I am very grateful to Shaun Khalfan and Doug Morgan for taking Salsa dance lessons with me as we tried not to step on each other's toes.

As my passion for partner dancing grew, I sought, through the encouragement of my mother, to take private lessons with a professional Latin ballroom dancer. I thank both Michael and Melissa Scott for opening the doors of their studio to me, helping me trust the dance floor and the journey of partnership dancing.

To my mother – thank you for your unconditional love, endless support and encouragement, and limitless belief. Special appreciation goes to my grandmother for her countless hours of devotion and immeasurable amount of pouring love. I love you both beyond imagination.

My brother, for all of your moral support, understanding, and creative energy. Thanks for loving me as I love you right back.

To my family, friends, my solo dance teachers, the dance community, and the business community who have embraced the merging of these two separate yet related worlds, thank you!

Thank you to those of you who have always jumped to support me and were by my side on this "Dance of the Business Mind" journey. You know who you are and I love you for it!

Thank you to my students and those I have mentored and coached over the years for giving me the opportunity to be of service.

Thanks to the angels who continuously and magically create opportunities and chance meetings to occur and make the impossible possible.

And thank you, Universe, for bringing to light that this is my calling and putting the pieces together for me in unexplainable ways. Thank you for teaching me to be patient, to let go, pay attention, and dance to the music that surrounds me and enjoy every moment of this journey!

INTRODUCTION

For most of my adult life, I've had primarily two great loves – by day, my business; by night, dancing.

During the day, in the conservative suits of a business consultant, I would work in partnership with many to transform, assess, strategize, and execute to deliver desired results. The partnerships that were formed came in different shapes and styles. Some partnerships were internal with employees; some partnerships were resources based on third party arrangements (outsourced services); some were with consultants or subcontractors, some were with vendors, and many were formed with clients.

At night, I would put on my ballroom practice shoes and flowy dance outfits to train and perfect another kind of partnership, with just one person: my ballroom dance partner/coach. We would go off to hone my roles as the cape, the bull, or the flamenco gypsy in the Paso Doble; work on my seductively dramatic leg flicks and action in the Argentine Tango; practice the proper bounce and body rolls for the energy of the exotic Brazilian Samba; perfecting our speedy steps in the playfully flirtatious Cha Cha Cha; and enhancing the sensually romantic connection of the Rumba. From time to time, we would perform in a show dance and compete in dance sport competitions.

I love both sides of my life. They both have led me to strengthen my passion for psychology, human dynamics, and the art of communication.

Then in my "daytime" life as co-owner of an executive consulting firm, I added another project: writing a business book called *The Four Intelligences of the Business Mind*. Just as I submitted the final manuscript, I found out that one of my dance role models, World Professional Latin Dance Champion, Yulia Zagoruychenko, was going to be in the Washington DC metro area. She would be performing and also offering a workshop and private lessons. I couldn't miss this event.

On the day of the event, I arrived early to register. While I was waiting for the event to begin, a charming man with a smile greeted me with an Italian accent. He introduced himself to me as Riccardo Cocchi, Yulia's professional dance partner. I was intrigued. We delightfully engaged in a conversation that led me to sign up for a private lesson with him. During the lesson he began sharing the importance of connection and coordination in partnership dance. In the middle of practice, we realized just how intertwined partnership elements in both dancing and business are. He looked deeply in my eyes and told me, "You really should write a book about this."

The next morning, as I was putting on my mascara, getting ready for another dance event with Riccardo and Yulia, the title of the book came to me. It was fate. A calling from the universe. I knew I had to do it. I rushed to find Riccardo, pulled him aside, and looked at the now seven-time World Professional Latin Dance Champion and said to him, "I'm going to do it!"

After I created an outline of what I wanted to cover, I did some research about the psychology and physiology of dance. Throughout the process I interviewed some amazing people to fill in the gaps, ranging from two of my own dance coaches to teachers, partners, judges and celebrities like Karina Smirnoff of *Dancing with the Stars* and Slavik Kryklyvyy who co-starred with Jennifer Lopez in the film *Shall We Dance?*, along with many other champions, adjudicators, sport coaches, representatives of dance council organizations, business leaders and entrepreneurs from the world of ballroom dance. Each clarified additional elements of partnership dancing that I found synchronous with business partnership. Arianna Huffington, co-founder and former editor in chief of *The Huffington Post* (now founder and CEO of Thrive Global) and New York Times #1 bestselling author of *Thrive* and *Sleep Revolution*, also took interest in my voice of blending the subjects as well as *Entrepreneur* magazine and others.

Though it uses dance as a metaphor, this book teaches you to use the methodology practices of my company, Acolyst. This methodology has been used in projects at many US government agencies, including my current one with the White House, Executive Office of the President of the United States (EOPOTUS). The world of business and ballroom dance have an awful lot in common.

My goal is to inspire others to approach their business with the same passion that is inherent in the dance world. I find that in both dance and business, passion comes from transformation – continually finding and succeeding at challenges that will let you expand who you are and what you are capable of.

In Chapter 1, "The Decision to Dance," you will set your intention to transform your business, then initiate the process to discover what transformation you are most passionate about making.

In Chapter 2, "Elements of Mental and Physical Preparation," you will gain insight into the current state of your business with regard to your future goals. Then you will identify what internal and external resources you already have on hand in order to begin to achieve the changes you want to make.

In Chapter 3, "Choreography," you will map and create your story; you will create a plan of action that brings you the opportunity to succeed in the best possible way. You will make sure that your "steps" (your business plan) match your "music" (your goal) as you forge ahead.

In Chapter 4, "Practice and Rehearsal," you will learn how practice, in business, executing your strategy through an internal test phase. You will report on what works and change what needs to be improved before you go through your full launch.

In Chapter 5, "Performing at Competition," you'll discover the ins and outs of seizing the opportunities you've been dancing towards, as well as the mindsets to employ just before, during, and right after your launch.

Finally, in Chapter 6, "Take Your Performance to the Next Level," you will learn how to evaluate your performance in the most positive way in order to benefit from it as you take your next steps. Did you succeed at achieving your transformational change, or did you somehow get stymied from attaining what you wanted? You will discover how to re-check, re-design, re-posture, and re-position for the future, no matter your results.

This book is one dedicated to practical actions, not theory. For you to get the full benefit, you must answer the questions that are posed and execute the items that are given to you to do.

Every step is important and will be useful to you. You will decide what it is you want to change, and then because of that, begin to see your business in a more complete way. You will engage in a transformative process that will lead you to exceptional performances and greater passion for what you do. And you will discover how changing your business will have a positive impact on your entire life, as the principles in this book work across the board for all that you are and do.

It really is fun and powerful.

If you read and act on every chapter, you will find just how pleasurable (and exceptionally thriving) it is to engage in *The Dance of the Business Mind*.

CHAPTER 1

THE DECISION TO DANCE

Take the Next Step to Transform Your Business

I fell in love with dance because of my mother.

That's not to say that Ellie Nazemoff had a one-track mind. Even today, she has a successful data consulting business.

But when she wasn't working, as a hobby, she would dance at home, at parties, and at family events. The Persian style dancing my mother did was a cross between belly dancing, hip hop, and modern and classical ballet. These dances hailed from a variety of regions. They were expressive solo dances that communicated messages, sometimes even spiritual ones, through graceful movements. She still has a way of connecting with herself and those who watch her – transforming through each transitioned movement.

When I got to college at George Mason University, I became heavily involved with the Persian club. I immersed myself in various aspects of dance and performance; learning and being exposed to the stage work, drama, choreography and performances of traditional and modern Persian dance routines. One of my performances for the Persian New Year involved putting together a team of sixteen dancers, eight men and eight women, which drew a full house of 1,200 people to a standing ovation. We were even invited by Penn State and Cornell University to perform at their campuses.

These performances were something that filled me with pride and passion. Dancing was about the ability to speak, communicate, collaborate, and bring to the spotlight a vision no matter the culture, gender, or type of person dancing. Some people came directly from Iran, some had lived in Germany (or other countries) and moved to America, and some were born and raised in America. No matter what experiences and prior exposures they had, everybody worked together to bring an amazing show and performance to life. Even though I was a young woman, I loved being theatrical and entertaining the audience. I especially enjoyed inspiring the audience to get up and dance.

As I graduated and evolved into an executive consultant, I discovered that I experienced the same feeling as back in college whenever I helped others to make decisions or coached them. The people I worked with experienced more than a business transformation; they experienced self-transformation as well. Clients became more confident and passionate about their work and better able to express creativity in their business dealings. They connected to joy when implementing changes, changes that previously might have felt stressful and more like a chore.

I began to view their newfound passion – which I felt as well – as a "Dance of the Business Mind."

It seemed to be the perfect metaphor for my goal of helping people achieve transformation.

To me, the "dancing mind" is a symbol for breaking through old psychological boundaries and attitudes that limit achievement, as well as for continuously moving towards new and exciting mental, physical, and spiritual beginnings leading to lifelong positive change.

A "dancing mind" represents the process of opening minds to new ideas, enhanced awareness, and a profound understanding of the deep forces and unseen interconnections within all of us – connecting with our deepest most inner value. To "dance" requires the synchronous presence and participation of your mind, body, and spirit, with spontaneity and centered awareness. Working from that state will take you on a transformational journey that leads to extraordinary performance in business and in life.

This journey begins when you empty your mind of all the overused or undernourished ideas you have about dance (or other sports), business, and living. By opening your mind and being receptive – which requires a particular mindset – you invite many new attitudes on which you can build your approach to all of life. You will see things in a refreshing, exhilarating way, and become aware of a multitude of alternative avenues that lead to extraordinary performance. This is your initiation into the eloquence and the grace of the "dancing mind," a state of mind that opens you up to your unlimited potential for achievement.

I refer to dance as both a metaphor for transformation and as an expression of passion and your values. Dance provides a visually dynamic and kinetic language so that you utilize your whole body and your mind as participants in a creative process.

Can the body think? It has its own special way of "thinking" when you cease to interfere with its deep-seated intelligence, known as instinct or intuitive physical response. Does the mind dance? It does when you free it to flow with life's natural processes and when you loosen your tendency towards critical judgment and control.

Being in a dancing state of mind means you realize that you have within you all you need to be and to do to make better business decisions, take action, and obtain results. It includes endurance, patience, persistence, fear, trust, reward, and success in ways that are applicable in any of the business life's demanding events. By learning effective strategies and techniques for dealing with these fluctuating states of mind in dance (or any sport), you will be better equipped to handle parallel situations in business and all of your other experiences.

Extraordinary performances and success in dance, as in all of life, are created by our passionate involvement in the moment; coming from continuous, mental and physical practice. The mindset of an exceptional dancer (or other athlete) is relaxed but focused. Real success or victory is measured by the quality of the dancer's attention and mindful involvement, practice, and commitment.

As human beings, we love this combination of relaxation and focus, where focus includes a readiness to take action. It's hardwired in our brains.

The hypothalamus, a region of the brain, regulates the autonomic nervous system (ANS), which is also known as the involuntary nervous system. This system takes care of ongoing bodily activities, like the beating of our hearts, digestion, and the rate at which we breathe, usually occurring on a subconscious level.

Within the ANS are the sympathetic (SNS) and parasympathetic (PNS) nervous systems. The PNS is in charge of rest and digestion. When it is aroused, it gives a calm and relaxed feeling in the mind and body. So the PNS responds to life with the calming feeling of watching ocean waves.

The SNS deals with perceived threats. It responds with an automatic sense for a need of fight or flight, either challenging whatever is causing the perceived threat or running away from it. The SNS creates a heightened sense of alertness, like watching the daring acrobatics at a Cirque du Soleil show with your pupils wide open.

The most satisfactory work life has a balance of stimuli to both these systems – so there are opportunities to feel both deeply at peace and on your toes.

This journey has no final destination because it is constantly evolving and transforming, thinking in new ways about how you work and play. By shifting your attitudes and beliefs about what is possible in your world, you will be able to redefine your potential, which really is unlimited, and unlock the extraordinary powers of your mind and body. Do that, and you will find your business has more meaning than you realized and you are living with a greater sense of your purpose and a sense of service to the world.

Passion

Dance, at its core, is passionate. Perhaps the most important challenge for any of us is to live our daily lives in the spirit of passion. By being true to your passion(s), you support and encourage your own journey, your attempt to make sense out of what you do and how you do it, in a world where most people doubt themselves and fear change.

If you are to live according to the "Dance of the Business Mind," you must invoke your passion by learning to listen closely to your inner voice. Doors open to those who follow their passion; and the world also moves to help those who live a life of authenticity, value, and integrity.

That's what happened to my former dance teacher and partner, who was a professional ballroom competitor.

His parents' dream was for him to be a world-class pianist. Being raised in the Soviet Union, he enrolled in dancing when he was six, to protect his hands from any injury that might come about with major activity and intense sports. Though he was successful in dance competitions in Europe and Russia as a child, when he came to the United States for college, he stopped dancing in order to focus on his piano training. Even though his studies kept him busy, he found that he was missing the action of the dance world.

But as luck would have it, he wound up working part-time playing piano to earn extra money for college – at ballet schools. And a funny feeling rose inside him. "I was jealous every day watching the dancers because there they were expressing their music with their body and I was just playing piano," he shared.

His envy became even more intense when he saw someone just going through the motions. For him, dance meant passion.

Between seeing that and a video of a championship ballroom dance, he made a decision: "I have to do this. I cannot NOT dance!"

That realization led him to a fulfilling career as a professional ballroom dancer and teacher who has gone on to inspire thousands in the world of dance.

YOUR Passion IS Your Purpose

The moral of the story is this: If there's something you're really passionate about, you need to express it in your work.

This book is an expression of the three subjects I am most passionate about: dance, psychology, and business.

When you must make business decisions or personal choices between what is practical and lucrative, what is efficient or effective or what truly is your heart's desire, go to a deep place inside yourself and ask, "Who am I?" "What do I really want out of this business or life?" and "Why is this important to me or to my customers or the team of people I work with or who work for me?"

These questions are how you identify what you are passionate about. Purpose gives meaning to the activities you perform and makes it easier to achieve success with them.

The "dancing mind" comes to life when it has a sense of purpose. Often that purpose has to do with an inner drive to express your talents, a desire to learn something new, or a need to be of service or inspiration to the outside world, which could be your customers, your employees, or the community at large.

For some people, their purpose and motivation comes from their need to express their "Business Mind." To use the "Business Mind" is a way of approaching business through the lenses of both the analytical and the intuitive parts of the brain. (I write about this in greater detail in my book, *The Four Intelligences of the Business Mind*). They enjoy being able to analyze where they are, where they want to be, and what it takes to get there. (Some common industry nicknames for these are the "as-is," the "to-be," and the "plan.") They like using their creativity and intuition to come up with ideas to leapfrog ahead of the competition. They get a kick out of analyzing their business and making incremental improvements to almost every area they look at. They are thrilled with the intuitive aspect of mentoring and in particular, when someone they mentor "gets it" and grows into a role that at one time was a stretch for them.

For others, the real joy comes from getting to do more of what they love. They are passionate about their talents, and they want more opportunities to express them – whether it's as a management consultant, a health practitioner, architect, or designer.

There's a third group of go-getters who are on a mission to have their product or service reach more people because they believe they have something better to offer than what's already out there – if only more people knew about it. These are innovative thinkers like the application developer who creates an organizational communication app that actually helps people stop procrastinating and gets things done through collaboration, or the alternative medicine healer who knows what herbs to provide to get rid of the flu within 24 hours.

Whether you need to express your "Business Mind," your talents, or just reach more people, the only way to move forward is to make a decision to join the dance – to proactively transform your business – in whatever way that will take you to the next level.

Your goal is to find something that you find so compelling, that you want to do so badly that you "cannot NOT do it" and incorporate that into your everyday work.

It doesn't have to be the whole ball of wax – it can just be a part of what you do. But that part will provide you with the satisfaction and fulfillment necessary to make your mind dance.

You may experience self-doubt from time to time, but your "dancing mind" will strengthen your resolve. You are a great spirit, and great spirits have always encountered and overcome resistance and obstacles along their way.

There's another important reason to do this: You want to put yourself in a leadership position, so you don't have to always react to what everyone else in your field is doing. A connection to your passion and purpose will bring you to a place where your work reflects the truth of who you are as a person, thus increasing your personal satisfaction and perception of innovativeness by your customers or clients.

Don't Just Learn How to Follow

A dance coach learned a similar version of this lesson when he was beginning to teach partner dancing and started by mimicking what he had seen other teachers do. The basic philosophy of dance at the time was that the woman follows and the man leads. "I spent a lot of time teaching the girls to follow," he told me.

This put a lot of pressure on the girls he taught.

"I did not realize how much it was affecting the girl," he adds. "She constantly had to be on her toes thinking, 'What's going to happen next?' Can you imagine a life living like this, not knowing what's going to happen and just being ready to respond to that every second?"

The solution is simple: "You do not teach someone to follow," he says. "You teach them to dance. My students, before I get them on the floor, I know that they can dance the entire routine by themselves."

It is the SAME in business. The reason you want to be mindful of transformation in business is so that you can be prepared and proactive and not depend on your "partner" for success.

Your Decision to Dance Will Lead to Transformation

That is why you need to make the decision to dance – to take action right now. Finding out and being self-aware of what gets your heart, mind, body, and soul to sing and dance in the workplace. Being self-aware is to be the observer of yourself and be aware of the awareness. But what do I mean by transformation? Transformation is about being mindfully aware and alert as to where to make changes. It has to do with a change that impacts people, processes, technology, and information. It's also about learning how to assess the impact of what you're hoping to do and evaluating the risk you will be taking versus your potential reward. This is true whether you want to grow your business, refine the model you are using, or make it more efficient and effective.

Deciding to make that transformation is one way you can lift your business to new heights. Transformation will allow you to undergo a metamorphosis, to evolve from one state of being to another. In essence, transformation is a mindset. It comes in different styles, shapes, and forms, ranging from creating a new product or coaching program, changing the structure or marketing of your business, defining and/or delivering your product or service in a new way, expanding to a new market, consolidating in ways that will save you money, or perhaps changing the entire direction of your business. Your transformation may have an impact on the people you serve and the people who work with and for you, how you do things, your technology, and even the information you use.

But your business won't be the only thing you transform.

An Added Benefit

Something unusual happens to me every time I create forward movement for my business: I also find that I have created forward movement for myself as a person – on the inside. I run Acolyst, a company that provides solutions for data management, business performance, information technology, and the ins and outs of working with the government as a strategist. A lot of my work has to do with helping others transform and execute.

It turns out, however, that when I achieve something new, it always transforms the way I feel about myself and then inspires me to take risks in my personal life. For example, I changed my business model so that I could accomplish everything I did before with more balance in my life, particularly paying attention to ways I could be more efficient through the use of the cloud and mobile apps. Oddly enough, these technical shifts changed something inside me that created the desire to focus more time on dance.

I've seen the same kind of personal improvements happen for my clients. After I help them make their business either more efficient, more effective, or simply a more enjoyable place to be, it's amazing to see how different they become as people. Some profoundly exude more confidence. For others, there is a sense that they are more relaxed – more in tune with themselves and the universe.

You'll experience this for yourself. Once you take action from a place of clear focus and direction, the environment around you changes. Your internal experience shifts as well.

Sometimes these changes come just from taking one small action.

My former dance teacher saw this same effect on his students. "I had this one lady who came in, she was very, very shy," he says. "She was sitting in the corner of the room and everybody who was passing by, she would lower her eyes and she would not even look up.

Even though she was afraid, she stayed. In spite of how shy she was, she had a compelling reason. At first she talked about losing weight, but that wasn't the real reason. 'I want to try,' she said. 'I want to see how it will feel.'"

There's a part of us that knows we need to grow and transform. That was certainly the case with this woman. After that first lesson, her formerly downcast eyes lit up with pride and she became so passionate, in a month she had become outgoing and social. She shared, "My work is improving, I'm now the boss of me, I feel like I can do everything."

So after that month, he asked her if she'd like to try a dance competition, and she instantly agreed.

Interest Versus Commitment

There was a reason he suggested a dance competition, aside from the allure of winning. "Sometimes I like to set goals for students to compete, mainly because it drives them," he says. "I have a couple of students who generally don't like competitions. They do it for fun; they just like dancing. The difference that I see between them and everybody else is that they don't grow as fast. No matter how much they work, there is no destination."

In ballroom dancing, a competition or show dance performance makes you more committed to the process.

If you want to transform your business, you have to make a commitment as well. You have to have a targeted goal.

You can't just be interested in making a change.

"There's a difference between interest and commitment," writes Kenneth H. Blanchard, co-author of the One Minute Manager series. "When you're interested in something, you do it only when it's convenient. When you're committed to something, you accept no excuses; only results." [1]

Or as business management guru Peter F. Drucker puts it, "Unless commitment is made, there are only promises and hopes; but no plans."

You can't just tiptoe into change, which is what many people want to do.

Though I tend to jump into everything with both feet, there are times when even I take the tiptoe approach. For example, as I write this, there's a flamenco event upcoming in Spain and I'm still deciding. I'm very interested, but I'm not 100% committed. I know this event will be inspiring and intriguing. I would learn a lot from it: the flamenco, the palmas, the tangos, and the dances from Seville. Even though I'm interested, I'm not fully committed to go. I can feel that hesitation within myself. Should I stay? Should I go? How would that impact my business?

---

1. ""Popular Quotes,"" Goodreads, accessed 2015-2016, http://www.goodreads.com/quotes/.

I know from past experience that once I make that commitment to go, I will find ways to reschedule my meetings for a week. I'll manage to meet urgent deadlines ahead of time. I'll get certain items off my calendar by delegating them to someone else. If I'm committed to go, I will figure out a way to make everything that needs to happen, happen.

The same thing applies in business. You have to make whatever will transform your business an actual commitment. Otherwise you will always stay in the same place you've always been. You need to say, "Okay, now is the time I need to improve our marketing." Or even more specific, it would be your search engine optimization (SEO), or your website, or your communication e-newsletters with your partners. If you don't prioritize it, you'll be too busy putting out fires in your normal day-to-day activities to ever make it happen – or to really give it your best effort.

The first step on your to-do list regarding the new matter at hand should be to communicate to the other people you work with. Even if you're a solopreneur, you have customers or clients, people you outsource to and/ or vendors, all of whom are affected by and who may affect your choices. Make sure that everyone's aware of this priority so you can all work together towards your commitment.

Before you add other tasks to your to-do list on this project, take some time to clarify what the mission, vision, goals, and objectives are for this initiative. What does it mean for you, your team, your partners, and anyone else involved? Now, explore what tasks are needed to achieve these goals. How you direct your focus is very important here. You can focus on task to task, work day in and day out, or you can focus on the accomplishment of something great. Notice how focusing this way helps motivate you to succeed.

When you know the importance of your role, are held accountable, and understand the significance of how your work impacts many, the motivation and enthusiasm to thrive increases (and procrastination decreases). When people come together with an attitude that the team needs to win, they overcome their resistance and go for the win.

You really have to actually take action, though, in order to succeed. Don't be one of those people who buys lots of business books and marketing programs, whose head is filled with facts and anecdotes about how other people have successfully increased their bottom line, but who never actually takes action for themselves. That won't get you anywhere.

Business is just like dance in this respect. Reading, watching or talking about it will never let you know what it feels like to glide across the dance floor.

Your Beliefs

If you've noticed you have a tendency towards being a wallflower and find you don't actually get on the dance floor and take action for yourself, there's something you can do to get your "Business Mind" ready to dance; examine your beliefs. These are not religious or philosophical beliefs, but rather self-concepts you hold about yourself, consciously or unconsciously. You may have one or two that are holding you back. Your beliefs can be a big influence on what you experience in life. Henry Ford said, "Whether you think you can, or think you can't, you're probably right."

Here are some questions you might ask yourself:

- What do I believe about what I can and can't achieve?
- What messages did I get about this from my parents, family, or superiors?
- Am I willing to see a bigger picture of what is possible for myself?

Really take some time to sit with these questions. You might even want to journal about them. The answers may surprise you. Some people are aware they have a belief that's holding them back. Others may not discover it until they take the time to think about it.

If you feel held back when taking action, you will eventually discover that your worst enemy is yourself; the greatest obstacle is your mind and its belief about what is possible. We often hear inside of us the voices of the people who drilled our potentially limiting beliefs into us from birth. For example, we are all born natural athletes, yet some of us are told as children that we are uncoordinated and clumsy. If we believe these labels imposed on us, we usually avoid physical activity; this avoidance then perpetuates the "un-athletic" characteristics, since we never give ourselves the chance to develop our physical selves. Even the best athletes and performers carry around internal sayings such as, "My backhand is weak" or "I'm a really slow runner."

Work on freeing yourself of these negative labels. Get in touch with the real athletic you. If you think you can't, then you not only sabotage your own beliefs but your own efforts to even try. You won't do what's required to realize the goal and make it come to fruition. When performers have negative thought patterns, they create mental and physical resistance that greatly hinders their performance.

Professional athletes are increasingly discovering the power of positive attitude and thought. That is why fans are important! Outer cheering creates inner belief. Inner belief creates positive outcomes. If you want evidence, look at your favorite team's home record versus their record during away games.

When you open your mind and believe you can, you forge paths of behavior and thought that help ensure that the dream will be fulfilled. You tap into a psychological state that creates dream fulfillment; it includes a mindset of hope, motivation, commitment, confidence, courage, concentration, excitement, and observation.

Affirm A Better Outcome

The words you use to express yourself plant the seeds of your future experiences. Positive attitude and thought are conveyed to the mind and body through the language of affirmations. (Affirmations are explained in more detail in Chapter 4.) Deeply ingrained beliefs or attitudes can sometimes be uprooted and changed by habitually choosing a different set of words to use on the topic.

Strong positive statements "make firm" what is already true or has the potential to become true. Since your achievement is usually a reflection of your images, and your images follow from your thoughts and words, it pays to construct a language of affirmation that complements the positive pathways of the rest of your behaviors. By so doing, you replace negative inner chatter and counterproductive mental tapes with a fresh, clear, helpful inner coach who can lead you to success.

I am not a huge fan of intense exercising, but if I have negative thoughts about it, then I cannot build my endurance, flexibility, strength, etc. Simply changing the statement, "I hate the elliptical" to "I love feeling more energized after using the elliptical" provides more physical strength and energy, resulting in a more powerful, natural performance.

Linking exercise to my passion for dance is another way to make working out more enjoyable and even fun. I need to exercise to tone my arms, increase my endurance, enhance my flexibility, improve my posture and balance, and engage my core. It even gives me a goal to work towards especially if I have a competition or show dance performance.

Try to discover aspects of something you detest that you can love, and focus on those. For example, many runners hate hills, but the difficult hills offer runners the opportunity to develop their strength and increase their heart's efficiency. It just makes sense to feel good about anything you're doing and to believe in yourself.

There is research that backs this concept up. An article in *Scientific American*, "Your Thoughts Can Release Abilities Beyond Normal Limits" reports on studies that show enhanced cognition, vision, and physical conditioning as a result of changing participants' thoughts[1]. In one study, two psychologists, Ulrich Weger and Stephen Loughnan, had two groups of people answer a series of questions that were to appear on a screen. One group was told that the answers would be flashed briefly before each question, too quickly to read but long enough for their unconscious to pick up on the answer. The other group was told that the flash was just an indication that the next question was coming. In reality, both groups were shown flashes of a meaningless set of letters.

Even though nothing of any consequence was happening, the first group, who believed they were receiving unconscious knowledge of the answers ahead of time, scored higher on the test than the second group, who just thought they were taking a test. The first group's belief that they knew the answers actually influenced how well they performed!

---

1. Atasoy, Ozgun, "Your Thoughts Can Release Abilities Beyone Normal Limits," *Scientific American*, August 13, 2013, accessed 2015-2016, https://www.scientificamerican.com/article/your-thoughts-can-release-abilities-beyond-normal-limits/.]

Imagine what the power of believing you know the answers could do for you!

Activate your concentration, confidence, and courage. Begin to believe and be optimistic that you can achieve your goal and be present in the current moment. This will be your ultimate power to alter your game and win. Hard negative opinions about yourself distort the truth about your potential. Rigidity will block your growth. Fixed mindsets obscure the unlimited boundaries of your potential. Keep your mind open.

If necessary, start by simply acting as if you can. Role play like an actor or actress. You will stop believing you can't. Learn to neutralize an extreme force with its opposite force. Fight fire with water; fight anger with love; fight "I can't" with "I can." Our ability to neutralize extremes gives us the power to alter reality.

Once you break an "I can't" barrier in one part of yourself – everything gets easier because you now know it is possible to make a breakthrough. Breaking a similar barrier on another issue becomes, well, if not a piece of cake, certainly a simpler, faster process. Oddly enough, this process can be seen across the population, not just one individual, in the outer world as well. Once one person breaks a barrier, other people believe they can break the same barrier and then do it.

Before Roger Bannister ran a mile in under four minutes on May 6th, 1954, experts said that a human being could not run fast enough to do that. Two months later, two more runners ran four minute miles. That limit continued to be broken again and again. Ten years later, a high school student by the name of Jim Ryun broke that barrier. It is so common to run a mile in under four minutes these days that you are not considered an elite runner unless you can accomplish this task; but a little over sixty years ago no one believed it was possible.

How many of us face obstacles or walls in the way of progress and let the belief, "I can't, no way," block our journey? We have to practice refraining from making these judgments and assume "I can" until we're proven wrong. As we approach and try these seemingly insurmountable hurdles, we just might discover the incremental steps we need to take to get over them.

This does not mean to ignore the difficulties of life's circumstances. Instead, balance the negative with the positive, and life's difficulties and seemingly negative occurrences often become lessons that show us how to forge ahead.

Find a Role Model to Emulate

Choose a person, perhaps a well-known athlete, performer, business person, or even an animal that possesses a quality or trait you'd like to emulate. Imitate them in all respects in terms of the areas you want to succeed in.

I practice this technique myself with regards to dance. I emulate ballroom champions, especially the winners of Latin competitions. I love the flamenco hand styling and intense character of Ina Jeliazkova, the spins of Joanna Leunis and the elongation of the legs, arms, and body of Yulia Zagoruychenko. I try to imitate them even though I have tons of work to do in order to make progress. I set the bar really high to push myself to achieve my goals to some extent. Even if I aim for the moon and miss, I know I'll still be among the stars. I pair myself with a combination of these amazing dance performers in my mind and during my visualization I imagine my movements being just like theirs – creating awareness through movement. Then, prior to any practice or performance, I act as if I am that model. It also provides a great visual for the coaches I work with to know what I am aiming for, and we are able to have discussions with consensus.

Positive Images

You are more likely to recall visual input to the brain than input from any of the other senses. Researchers realized this more than one hundred years ago and call it the pictorial superiority effect. John Medina, author of *Brain Rules*, writes, "If information is presented orally, people remember 10%, tested 72 hours after exposure. That figure goes up to 65% if you add a picture." [1]

---

1. Medina, John, "Worth a Thousand Words," *Brain Rules Blogspot,* December 10, 2009, http://brainrules.blogspot.com/2009/12/worth-thousand-words.html.

That's probably because the occipital lobe, the part of the brain that allows you to create a vision of something that hasn't happened yet, takes up 20% of the brain's capacity. It's found at the back of the head.

The brain is hungry for visual input. When you introduce positive images or pictures into your mind as a model for your actions, your central nervous system accepts them as real and your body responds to them. This means that if you rehearse an activity perfectly in your mind, the effect is the same as if you rehearsed it perfectly with your whole body. When you actually do the task you've mentally rehearsed, you feel as if you've actually accomplished it before, as you have, in your mind's eye.

So if athletes or performers can picture each movement of an activity, in a relaxed meditative state before they do it, exactly how they want it to turn out, there is a great chance that they will carry out those same movements during their actual events or performances.

This same approach applies to business. If you have to give a presentation to a group or make a sales call on an important potential client or negotiate on a mergers and acquisitions deal, picture yourself doing the best version of it you can imagine; you are likely to perform this at your highest level, achieving what you want more easily, effortlessly, and without stress. You have a targeted goal and a vision.

Upgrade the Image You Hold About YOURSELF

Part of positive thinking and visualization is having a positive self-image. Athletes and performers carry around a mental blueprint of themselves, based on a rigid belief system formed by past performances. All their actions mirror this image.

Most of the time, your performance is a reflection of how you see yourself. (In my case it is my belief that I have a strong ability to perform and shine on stage, but also that I need to work on my technique. I am not afraid of the performance or the dance floor; I have confidence and love the audience; but I know that I need to work on my dancing – like my balance, spins, and much more.)

You will experience a powerful new image by nurturing your inner, true self through the use of positive visualizations and affirmations through visual rehearsals using visual meditations. Do what hypnotists call a "skill rehearsal." Start by closing your eyes and progressively relaxing each part of your body from head to toe. If you want, you can imagine your favorite color in sand texture filling each part of you as you relax it. Then, visualize whatever action you want to perform happening perfectly. Take extra care with the aspects you are most uncomfortable with by visualizing them in slow motion. You can visualize other parts of your activity in fast forward mode. When you are finished, play it back one more time in fast-forward mode. Then create a short positive sentence, no more than 10 words, you can say to remind yourself of this visualization, such as, "My backhand is powerful, accurate, and effective." Your athletic performance will begin to mirror this new image rather than the more limited version.

As your performance improves, be sure to update your self-image by incorporating your newfound success into how you see yourself. When you set a record or have a new personal best, reset your image of yourself to reflect the new you. If you fail to do so, you will not continue to perform up to this new level; your results will vary according to your self-image.

Take a Daily Victory Lap

One way to upgrade your self-image is to make a practice of taking special notice of your achievements and positive experiences throughout the day. You can even write a quick three word note to yourself to help you remember them for later. Just taking these notes will provide lasting excitement and motivation.

You can get greater mental benefits if, either at the end of the work day or before you go to bed, you take 10 minutes or so to think about your "daily wins" and how they made you feel. How did they happen? Were they the result of good planning, strategy, interpersonal relationships, or proper use of technology? When did you feel completely lost in the moment and truly engaged in what you were doing? Jot down some notes. Then look for ways to carry those feelings and positive behaviors during the following day.

Over time, accentuating the positive becomes a habit, not just a falsely sunny disposition. You will be able to easily identify what makes you feel the strongest and most effective.

Try seeking out a trusted colleague or mentor to take this challenge with you. Commit to taking a small amount of time each day for three weeks. At the end of each week, discuss your observations and your progress. Rather than having a gripe session, you'll find yourselves focusing on the parts of the week that motivated and inspired you.

So instead of looking to crush the bad, seek to celebrate the good and accentuate the positive. This fresh outlook will brightly color your days and bring lasting, realistic change. People may even start to ask you how you stay so positive every day. You never know!

Celebrating the good releases serotonin in your brain. Serotonin is an "I feel good" hormone that contributes to well-being and happiness. Feelings of importance and accomplishment can trigger it. So if you aim to be aware of and acknowledge your achievements, you can also enjoy a chemical boost from serotonin.

Decide What to Transform with the Four I's

One of the best things you can do for your self-image is to make a commitment to transform your business. Just making this commitment, even before you take action, will bring you energy and help you see yourself in a new light.

But how do you decide what part of your business to transform?

The answer may lie in something I call the "Four I's," which is one of the guiding forces in my professional life. It's so important to me that I made it part of the mission statement for Acolyst, my consulting firm that I co-own with my mother. We use it as a way to approach every client who works with us. It allows us to bring passion and expertise to the relationships with the people who hire us.

Using the Four I's can help you bring your passion and expertise to the transformational decision you're about to make. Here's what they are:

1. **Intention** – In a constantly changing world, strive to take a step back, pause, and identify your intention for each challenge you undertake, rather than rushing blindly towards a goal. You want to make the optimal next move for your company. Summon up all your belief and passion about your work, so that you make a goal that is big enough, but not too big to accomplish in a reasonable time frame. If you are like most people, you are in business to make a positive difference. Keep that in mind as you set your intention.

2. **Initiation** – Keeping your intention, you have to become proactive in your search for an opportunity to transform your business. Explore what your best opportunity to improve is – and then take action to make it happen. You want to take your business to the next level. Focus on going above and beyond your previous levels of commitment to your company. You may be a pro at over-delivering on your promises to your customers, but a bit of an amateur when it comes to keeping promises to yourself. Now is the time to change that and over-deliver on your promise to yourself. Do that, and without question, you will be able to get to the next level.

3. **Innovation** – If you want to evolve, you need to innovate. Your goal needs to be one of embracing change of all kinds, using your determination and creativity to achieve results. Innovation, whether it is connected to new kinds of sales and marketing, technology, or even content-creation requires courage, but it is essential to goal fulfillment. So when preparing your mind to dance, ask yourself, "In what ways can I make my business more innovative?"

4. **Improvement** – As a competitive dancer, I know that my partner and I have to constantly improve. Set a goal of constant improvement for your business. Your transformational decision may simply be to take something you're already doing and make it better. Ultimately, improvement isn't just about making this one decision to dance. You want to consistently focus on new areas to optimize in your business. That includes both what you deliver to

your customers and what you do to improve in terms of your own bottom line. Continuing with the status quo leads to inertia and a lack of growth. There's always somebody else who will go the extra mile to reach out to potential customers – including yours. In today's world, you have to continue improving just to maintain your current level of success, let alone grow.

Set aside time to go through the Four I's with your team, or any other people you think of as resources. Collaboratively brainstorm and make a list of items that might make sense as a way to transform your business.

Find Inspiration From Others

A Chorus Line is a backstage Broadway musical about an audition for a show on the Great White Way. This Pulitzer Prize winner was based on a series of all-night group interviews with dancers. One of the questions that director Michael Bennett asked was, "What made you decide to become a dancer?" The dancers' real answers were used by composer Marvin Hamlisch and lyricist Ed Kleban to create the songs in the show. One memorable tap dance number is called, "I Can Do That." The title of the song is what the character named Mike says to himself after watching his older sister, Rosalie, tap dance. One day, when Rosalie can't make it to her dance class, Mike grabs her shoes and tights and attends in her place. The character keeps dancing and eventually becomes a chorus boy on Broadway, all because he said, "I can do that." And Sammy Williams, the actor whose story the song was based on, won a Tony Award for playing another character in the same show!

What makes you say, "I can do that"?

What kind of dance are other people or companies doing that might look good on you?

One way to find out what you might want to transform in your business is to find what inspires you, and do the same thing, not exactly like them, but in your own way – using your own style, your own voice, your own dance.

When you're looking at what's out there, don't restrict yourself to companies that are the same size as yours; think as big as you want. You could have a local juicing company and be inspired by Coca-Cola. Obviously, even if you have multiple stores, you're going to have to do things on a smaller scale than Coke does, being creative with your more limited resources. But that doesn't mean you can't be inspired to take your business to new heights by the actions of a Fortune 500 company. That's the secret of the "Business Mind;" it looks at situations from every angle, both analytically and intuitively, and resourcefully implements solutions that are appropriate for your company, no matter the size or stage.

Once you've figured out who and what inspires you, think about what kind of results you will get by emulating their particular routine. Will you achieve:

- Top of mind awareness from the customer base you desire?
- Reviews or publicity from the best periodicals in your field?
- More customers?
- A larger line of products?
- A bigger e-mail list?
- Higher search rankings on Google?
- Referrals from the people you think you should be getting referrals from?
- More and higher quality employees?
- Advertising on the Internet, in publications, on radio or TV?
- Additional revenue and higher profits?
- Something else?

Whatever result you are looking for will only happen if you bust a move and make a decision to dance.

How Do YOU Want to Inspire People?

There's one other way to pick an area to transform in your business. Reverse the question of inspiration. Instead of asking what companies inspire you, ask yourself what you want to do to inspire people, whether that's your customers, your resources, or even your community. What do you want to be part of your company's legacy to the world?

Imagine that a newspaper or the local news station will be writing an inspiring story about your company one year from now. What would the headline for that story be?

That simple sentence could be the source of your transformational idea. After all, inspiring others is part of the transformational mind. Think about what direction the impact you want to make on other people could make for your company. That direction could bring your business to a whole new level of success.

Your Biggest Roadblock

I recently led a business transformation workshop and posed a question that clearly hit a nerve. The business owners and executives in attendance seemed to shout out the same answer at almost the same time.

Let's pretend to play Jeopardy for a moment.

The answer given by my attendees was, "Not making decisions!"

Can you guess what the $2,000 question was? (We're in Double Jeopardy.)

If you guessed, "What is the #1 biggest mistake decision makers make when trying to transform?" you just won $2,000. If you give it some thought, it makes sense, doesn't it? In *The Paradox of Choice*, Barry Schwartz warns to "...beware of excessive choice: choice overload can make you question the decisions you make before you even make them,...." [1]

Value action over perfection. By now, you've hopefully made a decision to dance, committing to transform your business and stepping to the next level. You've probably come up with a number of ideas to choose from. Don't get too bogged down making your decision as to which area of your business you will work on. Remember to use your "Business Mind." By that, I mean use both your analytical side and your intuition to choose. There will be other opportunities to enact your other ideas in the future, and there's no such thing as a perfect decision except in hindsight.

---

1. Schwartz, Barry, *The Paradox of Choice – Why More Is Less.* New York: Harper Perennial, 2004.

Sheryl Sandberg displays one of her favorite mottos on the walls at Facebook headquarters: "Done is better than perfect . . . aiming for perfection causes frustration at best and paralysis at worst." [1]

My team and I are attempting to produce videos answering business management questions. "Vlogging" (video blogging) is a new endeavor for us and the initial videos have been far from perfect. The fact is that we could scrutinize and reshoot many times and still not achieve "perfection." However, we value the message as more important than the actual delivery, so we offer our imperfect best, with the trust that continuing the process will make us better over time. Our viewers have responded that they appreciate what we have to say, and to be honest, we've received no complaints about the video quality.

So come with me on this transformational journey. I assure you, you will enjoy stretching yourself. As one of my dance coaches once said, "The only thing that matters is how you feel when you dance."

In Chapter 2, I'll help you gain insight into where you are today in your business as well as determining what resources you already have, and which ones you need to add, in order to help you overcome the challenges you face.

---

1. Sandberg, Sheryl, *Lean In: Women, Work and the Will To Succeed*, New York: Alfred A. Knopf, 2013.

CHAPTER 2

ELEMENTS OF MENTAL AND PHYSICAL PREPARATION

The Insight and Preparation You Need for Business Transformation

Once you've established a transformational mindset, the next step is to gain insight into your current state and your future goals. Then, identify what resources you already have in order to begin to achieve the changes you want to make.

When you decide to embark upon a new project or initiative, it can be an exciting and stressful time. The upside potential can be limitless, but the roadblocks can seem daunting. That's when insight comes into play.

Insight is the capacity to gain an accurate and deep intuitive understanding of yourself and your business. You need a clear picture of how your resources and challenges stack up.

Painting an accurate and detailed "as-is" picture does not often garner the acclaim it deserves. Most business owners tackle new initiatives by taking immediate action and flying by the seat of their pants. But self-reflection is absolutely imperative in order to create a project plan that meets your business objectives.

Your next step will be to gather this information. With it, you will be able to prepare mentally and physically for the changes you want to make. This chapter is about discovering where you are today so you can make a successful journey to where you want and need to be.

How I Use Insight with Regard to Dance

One of my favorite dance styles is the Paso Doble. It is choreographed to demonstrate the dramatic movement of Spanish bullfighting, set to the music of the flamenco gypsy dance. To dance my best, I first need to mentally and physically prepare. It is even necessary to train to get in character of the female role for this dance, as I learned from one of my dance coaches, Yana Mazhnikova. I start by getting into the mood – listening to Spanish guitar music to help me craft a certain frame of mind. Then, focusing on the proper posture and frame for the dance, I keep my heels down on the floor and shift my weight towards the balls of my feet while I lock my knees. Next, I need to send my upper thighs forward by squeezing my glutes and tilting my pelvis forward. I stretch my spine up and contract my core, bringing my shoulders down to create a contra balance with positive forward movement. I hold my arms up in front of myself while I lightly push away from my partner, keeping the chest up, looking straight in front of me with my chin down. I remain focused on the character of the dance – which captures the essence of a life or death situation!

This mental and physical preparation is not limited to moments before competition or during practice. I make an effort to remain conscious of it throughout my days. For example, how I sit and stand – even while sitting at my desk writing articles for publication or reports for clients, I focus on bringing my shoulders down and adopting a battle-ready stance. I continue to listen to Spanish guitar music periodically to keep me in the mood.

There are actions I take to expand my posture, frame, stance and flexibility as I continue to physically prepare. I look at resources I already have. Something as simple as the doorframes in my house can be used to stretch and open my chest. I focus on what else I might have to help me, realizing that I have some stretch equipment at home, like a foam roller or stretch bands I used in the past with my personal trainer and physical therapist that I can now reuse.

At this stage, I keep my focus simple. This is not the point in time to seek external resources, like finding yoga studios to help me stretch or going online to find an ergonomic chair to help me sit better. That comes later. It's all about assessing where I am and what I have at my disposal to work with right here, right now.

In your business, this step is all about the right analyses in terms of where you currently are right now. It's also about using your intuition.

Develop Your Business Intuition to Gain Greater Insight

As mentioned in Chapter 1, the "Business Mind" looks at every issue that your company needs to address through two lenses. One lens uses logic and analysis. The other lens uses intuition.

Intuition is to implicitly "know" without the conscious use of reasoning and is important for anyone's personal development and understanding.

In dance, after you have learned through habit how to do something like the Samba's botafogo, volta, and whisk moves, you begin to rely on a natural sense of timing. Your actions will follow a natural path. Like dancing, when you repeat certain patterns and are comfortable with them, you start trusting and listening to your intuitive self when the choreography unexpectedly changes. It is an automatic response, unconsciously kicking in to help you dance around other couples on the competition dance floor. Sometimes you have no time to think, and analysis is paralysis.

In a fast-paced business environment you must also constantly be positioned to instantaneously respond. When you use the intuitive part of your "Business Mind," you swiftly assess a developing situation and know how to react and respond.

We all possess this instinct, yet few of us trust it to the extent that will allow us to be successful. To begin to develop this trust, you have to become aware of your mental and physical responses, which takes practice. Practice following your instincts, observing the outcomes, and seeing how you feel about them. When you cannot see or understand what is happening or developing in the moment, don't push for the answer. Instead, take a break, relax, become calm, and go with the flow of your intuitive self.

Sometimes the intuition-driven business decision may seem unconventional to you in terms of your traditional patterns and cause you to doubt. In this case, use the logical part of your "Business Mind" to determine if your decision has a good chance of leading to effective and impactful results. If the answer is yes, then go for it. If no, then reconsider what is dancing through your mind. Think about the learning process. What might you gain from your decision? What might you lose?

You will hear mentors often teaching high school students to go with their first answer when taking their college exams. Generally the intuitive response is the correct one. When we second guess ourselves, we are responding to the "but" that follows our gut reaction. Change your typical response so that you stick with the part of your decision that precedes the word "but."

Unlimited potential is unlocked when you choose to tap into your intuition. Let's say you need to make a critical decision as to whether you should bid on a new proposal. Your inner voice can help; it is your most reliable guide. Note that logic is based on the known; the potential value of untested scenarios is unknown. Using your intuition to go beyond the limitations of logic, when appropriate, lifts your business to new heights.

There are a number of practices you can use to strengthen the intuitive part of your "Business Mind." Here are three:

1. **Meditation -** Descriptions of meditation often speak about how it gets you in touch with the still, small voice within. This is your intuition. If you don't already know how to meditate, there are hundreds of ways available online. One simple way is to sit up straight and still for a few minutes and maintain a relaxed awareness of your breathing. Let your thoughts come and go without getting caught up in any particular topic.

2. **Breathing Exercises -** Breathing exercises are a way to center yourself and help you relax. They also enhance your receptivity to intuition. Typically, you practice them for ten complete inhales and exhales. Here are three popular variations:

   a. **Even Breathing.** This is the simplest one to do. Breathe in for ten counts, then breathe out for ten counts. Do this ten times.

   b. **Double Exhales.** Breathe out for twice as long as you breathe in. For example, if your inhale is for six counts, breathe out for twelve counts.

c. **Square Breathing.** Breathe in for eight counts. Hold fo
counts. Breathe out for eight counts. Hold for eight counts
continue by breathing in again. This is a particularly
technique to strengthen your intuition.

3. **Progressive Relaxation -** This is a technique where you relax
your body, part by part, from head to toe or vice versa. One way
to do this is to tighten the muscles of your feet, then relax them,
then do the same with your calves and continue to work your
way up your body until you wrinkle up your face and relax it.
If there is a muscle group you can't physically tighten, imagine
tightening it and then relaxing it. Another way is to imagine
pink sand filling your body from head to toe. When you get to
your shoulders, let it work its way down to your fingers and then
continue with your chest and stomach.

How to Overcome Fear

Sometimes when I'm just starting to work with clients, they want to skip the
insight step and move right into the execution step. When I explain that the
transformation process actually starts by taking a deep dive into the here
and now, I sense a nervous shift in energy. I've discovered that this drive to
focus on the future comes from the fear of seeing and accepting the present.

Fear is a natural part of business and life; it doesn't go away. It can either
paralyze you or motivate you. Fear is actually an acquaintance you must
acknowledge and embrace; it is neither negative nor positive.

We often feel fear when we are overwhelmed by the enormity of a task.
It could be performing triple the amount of our usual number of dance
routines or presenting to influential investors.

To set the stage for success, create realistic, challenging, short-range
milestone goals for yourself, or collectively do this as a team. The adrenaline
boost from hitting each milestone releases endorphins in your brain that
help you overcome physical-related fatigue and stress.

Since you are likely to achieve these goals frequently, your mind will
internalize that "I am a winner; I am successful; I accomplish what I set my

nd to do." Doing this will release serotonin (happy chemicals) in your brain and will build courage, confidence, motivation, and commitment for future directions.

And if you really want to prime yourself for success, reward yourself for a job well done, (or a positive attitude maintained) at different checkpoints in the process. The *anticipation* of a reward releases dopamine, another positive chemical, in your brain. You can even make a list of what reward will go with which goal. Pick anything from a coffee run to a favorite dessert or a guilty pleasure TV show – whatever motivates you. When I was in the middle of an especially hard dance practice, I pushed through in anticipation of the post-practice reward on my list – a massage.

Timing matters, too. Don't postpone the reward only until after achieving the big goal. Break the goal down into milestones. What will it take for you to get to that goal? Reward yourself with each met accomplishment. If I am getting ready for a competition, I don't wait until after the competition to reward myself. Rather, I build rewards into the entire end-to-end process.

Certain situations can spur counterproductive emotions, such as presenting to auditors, confronting an irresponsible employee or contractor, being interviewed by media, negotiating with a client, or handling a crisis. You need to reprogram your "Business Mind" through visualization techniques and affirmations to transition these unpleasant feelings into comfortable ones. These techniques will be discussed in Chapter 4.

Often we must deal with our fear of failure, based on how we believe society or our culture will evaluate us if we fail. Some dancers view failure as shameful, which not only creates unnecessary anxiety, tension, and pain, but sometimes results in dancers quitting altogether. Once we realize that failure is part of the journey to success – that it cannot be avoided – it loses its sting, which is often the sting of self-judgment. As Michael Jordan said in a Nike commercial, "I've missed more than 9000 shots in my career. I've lost almost 300 games. Twenty-six times, I've been trusted to take the game winning shot and missed. I've failed over and over and over again in my life. And that is why I succeed."

You will fail less if you get out of your own way. In the five different styles of dance that I enjoy for both performance and competition, the most important one to me is the Paso Doble I discussed earlier. The others I dance for fun are the ones I perform better. When dancing the Paso Doble,

I often feel my body tense up as soon as the music starts. But I tell myself to relax and just have fun, no matter what the outcome. When I relax, I am able to dance at my highest level.

Remember that fear can be helpful to you, alerting you to where you need to be careful and prepared. To release fear you need to gather insightful information. The known will help calm your anxieties and stress. Fear helps you plan the work and work the plan.

Why do we criticize ourselves? We are afraid to let ourselves down, which stops us from trying new things. Criticism is in our own minds. We often judge ourselves first, so we can avoid the anticipated sting of criticism from others. If we get in touch with that, we can stop worrying what others think of us and feel free to think bigger and pursue our dreams.

When we look at something that's not working, it doesn't need to be accompanied by a huge storm of self-criticism. What if we could see things that don't work as simply calling out for some kind of change, like a burnt-out kitchen light bulb? We don't say, "Oh my, the light bulb went out, there's something wrong with me and I have to beat myself up before somebody else judges me because it's dark in here." We get a new bulb from the pantry, stand on a chair, and change it. And voila, there is light once more.

Evaluate where you currently are in your business. The problematic areas are not failures. They are just an indication of places that need to evolve. Seeing those places will make it possible for you to improve them. You can't improve what you don't see.

You were not born on this planet to be perfect. Relax and welcome opportunities to go beyond your present level of performance. Reward yourself for identifying possibilities instead of being obsessed with negative outcomes. Know that both dancing and business are ever evolving processes that invite progress at each step; sometimes like the Cha Cha Cha, you need to take a few steps back to move a few steps forward.

Overcome the Fear of Success

Some people, including my own mother, have a fear of success. Well, she used to have one. When she won major contracts or had a successful day, her mind used to kick into a belief that "something might happen; after a victory there must be a fall." She became overly cautious in the belief that something was about to go wrong. And sure enough, something would go wrong. This negative attitude (even during her successes) was transmitted to her team. When someone inevitably made a mistake, she said to herself, "See, I knew it." Either she didn't believe she deserved the success or she believed that she deserved to have something go wrong. Whatever the case, her beliefs often became prophetic. The good news is that since she has been consciously aware of her mental thoughts and attitude, she has been able to control her emotions and reactions to fear, turning this around for her.

We always have a reason for our beliefs, no matter how crazy they seem. In my mother's case, she was told as a child not to smile – otherwise people would see happiness and attempt to take advantage of her. She had to find and see through that belief in order to break free of the resultant mental pattern, which was that something would go wrong after any success!

I, too, had a fear of success. For me, success meant more work and less time for my beloved hobby, dancing. I had to face my fear of professional success and alter part of our business model to create successful wins AND give me the time to dance and compete.

Visualize Success

Another way to combat fear of success is to spend time visualizing yourself successfully doing what you are afraid of. See yourself making the breakthroughs you need to make in order to accomplish these goals; then, notice how wonderful it will be to experience the accomplishments that will result from pushing your limits.

In business, it is important to communicate the goal and have everyone visualize the breakthrough to get there as a collective whole. This technique is called "group consciousness." Neuroscience researchers, Dr. Andrew Newberg and Mark Robert Waldman, explain that group consciousness neurologically bonds you in socially positive ways and absorbs greater energy. That is why meditation and prayer practice in groups have more impact.[1]

---

1. Newberg, A. B., & Waldman, M. R. (2016). *How Enlightenment Changes your Brain: The New Science of Transformation*, p.238 New York: Avery.

Understand Your Strengths and Weaknesses

In dance, you are constantly being asked to look at your strengths and weaknesses. Strengths are nice, but one of the best ways to grow is to truly understand your weaknesses.

Here's an example from my life as a ballroom dancer: In the Rumba, you need to "be sensual" with your partner, audience, and judges in order to achieve the full impact of the dance. I was told that this was not one of my strengths.

At first, when I heard this criticism, I was indignant and defensive. But I had to listen with openness and realize that my coaches and partners were giving me constructive criticism and feedback in a non-judgmental way. I made myself stay open-minded and listen. Then I asked, "Okay, what do I need to do to be sensual?"

When they told me, I took their advice, did the work that was suggested, and I got a lot better.

As vulnerable as I felt being told to work on something as basic as being sensual, I needed to hear it. It was the only way I could find out something I *really* needed to know.

You need to be willing to be that vulnerable when you look at your business.

It's important to look at your own strengths and weaknesses and then to ask someone else (or several people) what they see.

Think about everything you do in a three-month period. What do you like to do? What do you hate? What are you good at? What needs improvement? What are your strengths and weaknesses?

Be open, accepting, and true to yourself when you ask these questions.

Use a Second Set of Eyes

No matter how honest you are with yourself, sometimes there are things you just can't see until they're pointed out to you.

I have a friend who just lost 75 pounds after someone posted a picture of her on Facebook. She said she didn't realize how overweight she was until she saw that picture. She knew she needed to lose weight, she just didn't realize how much until she viewed the evidence on social media.

That's why it's important to get an outside perspective. Talk to a mentor, a coach, a friend or colleague who you trust and can respect. Ask for non-judgmental feedback on what your business weaknesses are. Share your goal of becoming more aware of your weaknesses, so you can anticipate them and prepare to improve on them. This way, you'll be able to turn these weaknesses into strengths.

Receive their feedback with the understanding that it's constructive criticism. Take what they say to heart and listen without judging yourself.

As a dancer my strengths are my personality and confidence. I might not dance as well as some, but I'm very confident and I don't mind being in the spotlight. I love that.

Judges don't just look at your feet and your posture. They also look at your skill as a performer. You could be a great dancer, but not smile or make eye contact. You could just stay inside your own world and not remember to perform.

I know I need to work on my technique and my actual skill, but when it comes to my performance level, confidence and stage presence, I'm fine. Actually, I'm more than fine. People tell me I'm fun to watch. Even if I mess up, it adds something fun and lively to the show. For other people it could be the opposite – they have great technique but they don't connect with the audience and judges, so their performances are less compelling.

One more thing: Ask the person advising you to tell you about your strengths as well as your weaknesses. You spend so much time looking at what's not good, it's nice to have something positive to celebrate as you take your bow at the close of your performance!

Understand the Judges

If you don't know the basics of what the judges want at a dance competition, you won't even know what to pay attention to when watching. Many professional dancers see coaches regularly to help them improve the areas that they will be judged upon.

In business, you have to know what your judges want as well.

Who are the judges? They are your clients or customers, business partners, and even vendors and employees (they're judging you, too!). Make a list that answers the following:

- What do you believe others think are your weaknesses?
- What do you believe others think are your strengths?

Turn the paper over and answer:

- What do you think your weaknesses are?
- What do you think your strengths are?

Accept your shortcomings, accentuate your strengths, and focus on whatever is of value to you and the marketplace. These three actions are what it means to become aware.

If you don't understand what the marketplace values, you run the risk of getting good at a skill or creating something no one really wants or cares about. This happened to Apple with the Apple Newton, the old pen computing tablet. If you haven't heard of it, there's a reason why – it never sold well. It was so forgettable, I had to look up what it was called. The iPad, however, came out of a consumer and business need to have something bigger than an iPhone that could be used for work and leisure. It was something that both the business community and the consumer world eagerly awaited, and its sales, as well as those of all the other tablets, continue to reflect that.

What's Unique About You?

In dance and business, it's important to have your own personal flair, something that sets you apart from the rest of the crowd.

When Polina Pilipenchuk, a former six-time national champion and world finalist in the 10-Dance, (a rigorous competition where you dance ten different styles), is also a respected judge at competitions around the world, judges a competition, she sees every couple as different in the way they perform and interpret each dance. "Some couples, the level of their presentation and expression, they create something within you," she says.

"When you look at them, you just like them because you are becoming a part of the story they are telling you by using their body language. These couples are very unique in the way they dance."[1]

I recently discovered a way to add a pinch of panache to my dancing. I took the flamenco hand styling that I recently learned for the Paso Doble and started sprinkling it into all my styles. This adds a Spanish flavor, particularly with the Rumba, the Cha Cha Cha and the Samba. Even though I'm dancing the other dances, I have my own style. It's something unique that sets me apart from the other dancers.

You may already be doing something unique without realizing it. Maybe it's something external that people can see, or perhaps it's just something about you and the way you interact with people. Whatever it is, consider doing more of it. It's a resource you can use in your marketing or in your product or service. You just need to realize you have it.

That's why you should ask the person advising you, "Have you noticed anything unique about me or my business?"

You may be surprised with the answer. On the other hand, they may not have anything particular to say.

If it turns out to be the latter, try to find something different you can add to your marketing or to your product. With your marketing, look at other people as models, but use what they do as a point of departure or a way to generate ideas; don't assume that what they are doing is a right fit for you, your business, or the timing of it. If you constantly look at other people and say, "Oh, they're doing more videos or they're doing better social media" and then rush to do the same thing, you may wind up going in directions that are an unsuitable fit for you. Imitation can cause you to lose what makes you unique. Be conscious and weigh out the pros and cons.

What's Inside You is Your Most Valuable Resource

Make sure you keep an open mind, or as they say in Zen, a beginner's mind, as you look at each item you are reviewing. Leadership author and coach, Michael McKinney says, "What we know often blocks us from what we

---

1. Polina Pilipenchuk. Interview by author. Recording Virginia / Maryland. October 2015.

need to see." [1] A friend of mine had a mug with the following quote by legendary basketball coach John Wooden that also applies: "It's what you learn after you know it all that counts."

The Best Insights Come from a Relaxed Mind

It's important to let yourself feel as relaxed as possible during these stock-taking exercises. Don't let yourself become anxious about what you discover, even if you find out there is a need for a LOT of improvement.

Anxiety actually limits our capacity for ideas. This limited capacity is a positive evolutionary trait. If you were a cave woman who was in grave danger, having accidentally found yourself at the foot of the lion's den, you wouldn't want your brain to give you too many choices. You just need to make a decision between fight or flight, and fast. Too many alternatives would keep your mind so occupied that you would freeze and wind up as the course du jour for the lions.

No one is going to eat you at your office, so you can afford to relax and use the full capacity of your brain. When you focus your breath and relax, you can see your way clear to establishing a firm footing for action.

Even if you're not anxious, it's important to do things that help you relax throughout the day. Waldman says daydreaming and mind-wandering are vital for learning and maintaining a healthy brain. "If you take a couple of 'daydreaming' breaks each hour – just closing your eyes and letting your thoughts and feelings wander to wherever they want to go – you'll feel completely refreshed after a minute or two. Daydreaming is an essential process for encoding new information into long-term memory, and it also stimulates the creativity circuits in your frontal lobes." [2]

In dance, it's important to include a sense of physical relaxation simultaneously with your focus on your strength. The relaxation keeps your heart's arterial pathways open for better circulation, and your lungs expand to increase your oxygen consumption. Your muscles become more flexible and fluid.

---

1. McKinney, M. (n.d.). Quotes on SELF-DISCIPLINE. Retrieved November 2, 2015, from http://www.leadershipnow.com/disciplinequotes.html

2. Waldman, M. (2014). *10 Mind Blowing Discoveries About the Human Brain: NeuroWisdom and the Secrets to Happiness and Success*, p.9. Retrieved November 11, 2015, from http://launchmoxie.com/neurowisdom/

One of my trainers taught me an experiment that allows you to feel the difference your body experiences when relaxed. First, do some push-ups with your arms tensed, then do a few with your muscles relaxed. You will immediately see how much more effective the relaxed push-ups are than the ones you've done with your tense arms.

The implication for this is simple but powerful. You must relax in order to achieve your max.

What Judges Look For

You're always being judged by customers, partners and even your employees. Once you know what you are being judged on, you can analyze your company's strengths and weaknesses with an eye to meeting expectations that will help you improve your bottom line.

First, let's take a look at the world of dance.

Polina says that every judge has a tremendous amount of experience and knowledge dancing, teaching, and coaching. This experience influences what they are looking for. "As a judge we're not trying to understand what the dancers intentions are," she explains. "We would like to see the picture which they create. If this picture, according to my understanding of dancing, is right, then I like them. I look at the way they move, and the way they look, and what kind of silhouette they have as they move from step to step." Polina says that the judging starts with how the dancers present themselves as they walk in. "You can see the way the dancers carry their posture, and the level of confidence right away. We also look at the way they groom, everything. It's the whole package."

In business you deal with the same thing. You are being evaluated from the moment people interact with you.

In ballroom, judges begin by focusing on three main elements: *beauty*, *musicality*, and *partnering*.

1. **Beauty** in dance is about making the way you move look beautiful. As you work on a new dance, you start from the bottom and work your way up. It is not possible to learn everything at the same time. There is a learning curve. Once

you learn the choreography, your coach will address different aspects of your performance during each session. What you work on needs to be manageable. That is the key to progress.

Everything is connected, but it is helpful to understand what the judges look at, body part by body part:

a. **The Feet.** The feet are the foundation. "Every dancer has to develop good footwork," says Edita Daniute, World Professional Standard Dance Champion. "To maintain your position, frame and a better body line, you need good footwork. That's how we control our movement. Bad things happen when you start to lean or fall." [1]

b. **Leg action.** Next, you work on your legs. The goal is to make your walking – and all other leg movements – graceful and lovely. Edita adds, "First you make it look nice and then you time it correctly. You move the leg on time. That makes you look, not only pretty, but also fast. Because when you move on time you get there fast, like in the Quickstep which is about speed and lightness."

c. **Hips.** The movement in the hips is a reaction to the change of where you are placing your weight. You don't focus on moving the hips. The hips move because you move.

d. **Chest.** The chest is the center of your body. The chest helps create balance, emotion, and drive. This is where the heart is. One of the features that judges and even audiences notice the most is when your chest is not in proper position with your partner.

e. **Arms.** The arms are for styling, flexibility, and balance. When you do a spin, your arms help you stop. The arms help grab and focus the audience's attention.

f. **Head.** The head helps you know what direction you are moving in or what direction you are changing to. It helps you focus. The beauty of the head is manifested in your facial expression, confidence, relaxed, elegant, genuine look, and determined focus.

---

1. Edita Daniute and Mirko Gozzoli. Notes by author. Workshop and lessons. Virginia. January 2015.

2. **Musicality** in dance has to do with your sensitivity and receptivity to the score that is playing while you move. It functions like an additional partner. Musicality is about expressing sound with your body. You have to be on time to the music and let it affect you and your phrasing.

3. **In partnering**, the judges want to see you demonstrate dance positions, as well as your ability to transition from one position to another. This shows off your lead-follow communication. There's also the matter of chemistry between you and your partner – the connection. "How do you feel your partner, how do you touch your partner and express emotion through the body," says Vibeke Toft, former World Professional Latin Dance Champion. "I don't like the term hold. I like the term 'touch.' You touch with your whole body, including your eyes. At the end, all of these aspects are supposed to build an enjoyable experience. That's the feeling you want to leave with when you're dancing. If you can make other people feel what you're feeling and if it's nice, they will enjoy it. That kind of interaction between two people is very inspiring and that's what's beautiful." [1]

How Ballroom Expectations Apply to Your Business

What the judges look for at dance competitions have correlations in the world of business. Here's how ballroom expectations match up with what companies need to bring to the world:

Beauty is your style – your expression and who you are. It's your authenticity. The basics that the judges look for are the beauty of good posturing and presentation.

In business, customers, vendors, potential partners and employees want to see that you have a nice stable foundation and that you are walking in the right direction.

1. Vibeke Toft and Allan Tornsberg. Notes by author. Workshop and lessons. Virginia. April 2015.

As you work on the different parts of your body in dance, you start at the bottom and work your way up. In business, you have to do the same thing. As you move to a new level with your organization, you need to use a step-by-step process that allows for progress. Each step will be connected to previous and future ones. But just like in dance, the changes you make should be in manageable chunks that create an overall impact.

Musicality in business symbolizes the fact that you are collectively in this together. In dance, music keeps you connected. When you cannot see each other, music is what keeps moving in time to the same beat. Music is a universal language, and you have to remain aware that everything you do in your business affects and impacts the community and industry that surrounds you. Musicality also represents timing, as music is what provides the beat that you dance to. In business, this means keeping in step with the times and with your customers' needs.

Partnering in business requires the same flexibility as it does in dance. You go through a variety of dynamics, one after another, just as you do in terms of the physical positions in dance. Like closed, open and promenade dance positions, you show different sides of yourself as you exchange energy and ideas with your clients, business and joint venture partners, vendors and employees. It's very important for partners to help each other look good. Help your partner shine instead of hogging the spotlight and making it all about you.

Judgments People Make About Your Business

When you are mentally and physically preparing yourself for transformation, there are a few other things that people evaluate when looking at your business:

1. **Your Image/Brand** – What kind of image does your business present? Your brand encompasses everything that is communicated to the world about your company, including:

    a. **Your Website.** Is it professional and up-to-date? Is it mobile-ready? Is it optimized for SEO?

    b. **Your Print Materials.** Do your business card and your brochures represent who you are today?

    c. **Your Email Signature**. It's a little thing, but it does represent you. Are you using it to its best effect?

    d. **Your Blog.** If you have a blog, have you posted in the last month or quarter? Or are all your posts three years old?

    e. **Your Clients and Their Testimonials.** Testimonials are an important part of your website and/or your print materials. Are your testimonials up-to-date? Do they help you overcome the objections that potential customers have when they are considering doing business with you? Do they help you stand out from the competition? If you are in a business, such as government contracting or financial planning, where you can't post testimonials on your website, what you can do instead is to make sure you have clients who are referenceable.

    f. **Your Champions.** Are they creating the right kind of word of mouth for you? Also, are there some new people you haven't reached out to as possible character references?

    g. **Your Employees.** The people on your team are crucially important. Your employees give you strength. Your people are your voice. Are they positively impacting the customers and vendors they interact with?

2. **The Quality of Your Product or Service** – Have you ever taken a good, hard look at what you're delivering to the marketplace? Hopefully, you're in good shape here, but sometimes quality slips. Is your product or service up-to-date? Are you using the latest technology? Are there steps that you've known you've needed to take, maybe even for years, that you've let fall through the cracks?

3. **Your Integrity and Trustworthiness** – Do you deliver what you promise? This doesn't just apply to your clients or customers; it's also important in terms of your vendors, employees, and your joint venture partners. Are you paying employees and vendors on time? Do you communicate openly? Are you providing the opportunities you said you would? Are you delivering needed materials when they are expected?

These are some of the main things your business is judged upon. There's also another way the world is grading you that I haven't spoken about yet.

Judging Outside the Ballroom

Whatever niche your business is in, as they say in the Disneyland song, "It's a Smal World." Word gets around fast in small worlds. Ballroom dancing is also a small world.

The judges have eyes and ears everywhere. News travels fast. They hear about up and coming dancers and who's going to be competing almost as soon as the thought enters the dancers' heads.

Judges judge you even before you hit the dance floor because they've either interacted with you or know someone who has.

I run into judges at other dance studios and at competitions where I'm a spectator, but not competing. I also sometimes observe other dancers and how they relate with the judges. Some behave in a condescending, snooty way, causing the judges to look down on them. Some people are graceful and nice. I've noticed that they are the ones who wind up with better scores. Believe it or not, your behavior around the judges *off* the ballroom floor affects your dance score when you're on it. The judges are human beings and as humans, they can't help but be influenced on a subtle (and sometimes not so subtle) level by how they feel about someone.

There's also a word of mouth factor. People talk. You don't have to be on *Dancing with the Stars* to be judged before you're actually on the ballroom floor competing. Your hair stylist or one of the others at your salon may be friends with a coach or a judge that you don't even know about and say something about you. A dance studio owner might make what seems like an innocent comment in passing that may affect how the judges perceive you. You need to be consciously aware of the image that you are portraying everywhere you go, particularly with anything even remotely related to the dance world. Today, there is the "word of digital touch effect" where news and comments that can affect your reputation are instantly shared on social media and the Internet.

The same thing is true in business. If you have a meeting set up with a potential client, that person is already judging you before you have the chance to say "hello." I was on a conference call recently with a Navy captain. She had done a ton of research on us. She knew about my book, the periodicals and websites where I was being published, my next speaking engagement, and even other clients I had. She was on top of her game. Fortunately, she liked everything she saw and it helped her view me and my company as experts on a very specific topic that was important enough for her to want to engage.

But you never know. You have to be aware of what is out there about you on the Internet (including the ever changing social review apps like Yelp, if it applies to your business), in the media, as well as what people are saying about you in person.

Clients and customers are watching you. They are experts in the field. They know what they are looking for.

As a customer, let's say I'm going to Best Buy and I already know I want to buy the latest smartphone or fitness tracker. Before I hit the sales floor, I have an opinion. The media has expressed their ideas to me, my Facebook friends have shared their experiences, and I've already done some research and comparison. Before I go to the store, I have an image of what I want. So that Best Buy representative has very little leeway to sway my choice – I'm already pretty far along in my decision process before I step into the store.

Your customers do that same thing with you. Be aware of that in advance in order to help them see you in the best light possible.

Before we proceed, I'd like to offer one caveat. Is it important to take the opinions of others seriously? Yes, most definitely. But, you must keep things in balance, neither allowing good or bad opinions to influence you and your actions too significantly. The key takeaway is that people and customers are watching you, so make sure that you're giving them something good to watch and share.

Question Your Values

Another way to gain insight has to do with your values. Is your business living up to them? Do others share your core values in the workplace?

These queries are simple, but they can help you communicate your values and decide on what and how you need to work together:

1. **Are you doing what you really want to do?** I'm not talking about your overall business or career. Sometimes you get so waylaid by grabbing for the lowest hanging fruit that you don't get to do what you got into your line of business for in the first place. There is a dance professional I know who originally started training amateurs to compete, but she has been so successful obtaining clients who want to improve their confidence and do better socially that she doesn't have time to focus on her initial passion. She had to re-evaluate her personal values to re-focus her business on what she originally wanted.

2. **Are you able to help and serve others? Are you in business to make a difference? And what are you making a difference on?** It could be anything, but it's got to be true to you. Yana, is multi-talented. She is not only a professional dancer and teacher, but she also designs and makes luxurious couture dance competition dresses and is a ballroom-specific hair and make-up artist. She really enjoys helping others express their beauty and character; it shows in her attention to detail as she painstakingly matches everything from the stones in each dress to the hair and make-up for each of her clients' performances.

3. **Are you making a difference for your employees and others?** This doesn't need to be huge. For me, it's making sure I am able to create opportunities for others to put food on the table for their families and buy nice birthday and holiday presents for their children. I am also committed to guiding people who want to grow their skills and abilities. The difference that you make for others does not have to be grand. It can be simple and still be meaningful and worthwhile.

The Value of Knowing Yourself

By now, you might be saying, "This is a lot to think about."

If so, you are right!

But every ounce of energy you put into this process yields a pound of return, so keep at it. Getting a detailed, comprehensive picture of yourself *before* you take action on what you see, leads to the greatest success at transformation.

When you don't take stock of where you are, it's like having a 1000 piece puzzle without a picture on the cover to show you what the end product looks like. You have to figure out what goes together, without having a clue as to what you're looking for. If I were to show you even a piece of the picture, you would be aware of what to look for in terms of color and image. Out of a thousand pieces, you would be able to pick up twenty or so that could easily be a match. Your mind would be alert and ready to look for something specific; this particular part of the puzzle would be more easily solved.

Once you know and accept what you see about yourself, your mind shifts to a specific alert mode. You are prepared for what needs to happen in your business, and you will see opportunities that you wouldn't have noticed before. It's like when you are thinking of buying a BMW. Suddenly you notice all the BMWs on the road. Before you started thinking about a new car, they just blended in with the rest of the vehicles driving by. When your mind is focused, however, you notice what you have become alert about.

Therefore, if you become aware of what it is you need to transform, those items will be more easily transformed. That's one of the reasons for this process.

Your External Transformational Resources

Now that we've covered all your internal assets, it's time to identify what external resources are available to help you gain insight in preparing for strategy planning and execution.

Everyone needs external resources to aid them in their journey. It takes a village to build a company. It's not a one-person show. It's a journey with a team of people. Acknowledge them. Be grateful for them. Many times you're going to help them on their journey as well. Life, in general, is a partnership. It's a dance!

When Oprah Winfrey was starring on a local TV show in Chicago, she wasn't sure whether or not to take an offer to go into syndication with King World. She was afraid that if her syndicated show didn't work, in three months she'd be out of a job. Roger Ebert, the famed film critic of *Siskel and Ebert at the Movies*, was one of her external resources. He had been a guest on her program. And *Siskel and Ebert* was a syndicated show, so he possessed valuable experience. According to Ebert's blog of November 16th, 2005[1], they were on the second of their two meets.

Ebert gave his advice to Oprah on a paper napkin. He showed her, based on what he earned in a year, how much money she would make on her show, on a line-by-line basis. Since Oprah would do her show alone instead of with a partner, she would double what Ebert earned. The show would be twice as long, so her fee would double again. It would appear during the week and be at least twice as popular as a Saturday afternoon show of movie reviews, so she could double his original figure a third time. Finally, it would appear five times a week, so she could multiply the whole new figure by five. Ebert wrote down how much she would potentially make. The total was forty times (2x2x2x5) the amount he was making.

Then, he wrote, "I pushed the napkin across the table. Oprah studied it for 10 seconds. 'Rog, I'm going with King World,' she said."

And with that, television history was made.

You don't need to be Oprah or to have been friends with the late Roger Ebert to make good use of your sounding boards. Just be aware of what and who they are, and take action.

In dance, understanding what external resources you have is easy. Your main resources are your coach, the people who do your styling, the individuals who help you with your costume or outfit, the owners of nearby dance studios, and the people who come to support you when you perform.

Categories of Accessible External Resources

In business, there are some external resources everybody has and others that are unique to you.

Money is obviously a resource in business, and yes it is external. Why? It needs to flow. Money is a transaction. Since it's an important one, you need to get clear about the truth of your current financial situation. At this stage, we are only gaining insight into the "as-is" state.

1. Ebert, R. (2005, November 16). How I Gave Oprah Her Start. Retrieved November 01, 2015, from http://www.rogerebert. com/rogers-journal/how-i-gave-oprah-her-start

Where are you financially? Be realistic and accept where you're at today. How much do you need to keep in reserve as a safety net? After that, what money is available to transform your business?

The next most obvious external resources are your contractors and consultants. Know the difference. Contractors essentially act as temporary employees to help with a specific task that you assign to them, which you typically want them to complete in a particular way. What kinds of things do they know or have talent at that you currently do not have in-house?

Consultants, on the other hand, are usually hired to analyze situations that need improvement with a point of view from outside your company. Their task is to figure out how to make problematic areas better. What can they do to further your quest to transform? What information are they privy to from the people they interface with that might be useful for your business?

Other external resources most people have are their vendors and suppliers. You can ask the same questions about them as you did about your contractors, plus one more: Who can they introduce you to that might help you reach new markets, such as consultants?

At this point, you don't need to look for a specific task they can help you with. You just want to bring your awareness to the resources they could potentially bring. Those resources will then be top of mind when you're looking for help.

Who else are you partnering with on this journey that might be an external resource for you? Who are your cheerleaders? Who are your champions? Your influencers? For example, you might be selling jewelry. One of your fans might be a costume designer who believes in what you're doing because you have done something cool or you've been creative with a particularly beautiful design. She could create a lot of word of mouth for you and even share your designs on social media.

Don't overlook those that believe in you. This group of supporters might be people who come to most of your seminars, buy all of your products, or be impactful bloggers. David Meerman Scott, author of *The New Rules of Marketing & PR*, tells the story of Cindy Gordon, vice president of new media and marketing at Universal Orlando Resort. [1]

---

1. David Meerman Scott, *The New Rules of Marketing & PR* (New Jersey: Wiley, 2007), 282-285.

Gordon was tasked with creating a global marketing campaign for the new "Wizarding World of Harry Potter" theme park at Universal Studios. Warner Brothers could have spent millions of dollars, but instead, Gordon found the seven most influential bloggers and fan site operators for Harry Potter, connected with them, and engaged them by inviting them to a private screening. These seven initial influencers then communicated with the rest of the world via blogs and websites that had an estimated reach of 350 million people around the world.

In the dance world, your support group is the people who come to see you compete. It really makes a difference. Acknowledge the support you get in your business as well. For me, there were people in the media that were fans that followed and would praise our growth; there were also influencers who would praise my company at events and introduce me to key players they knew; and there were others that wanted to associate with me because we were like-minded and held similar values. Don't ever feel like you're too strong to need support.

I once was invited to speak on motivation at a body building competition. (I have to say that I was very motivated – they were really built!) Competitors go through months of disciplined diets, intense workouts, and extreme dedication to what they are attempting to achieve. Everyone who was on stage had their own group of supporters made up of their family members, friends, and co-workers. It was surprising just how loud each group of supporters could be.

We all need that – even in business.

Who will really support you through your journey? There are some people who will bring you down and won't believe in you or support you. Get rid of those people. Sometimes you can't, because it's your spouse or your brother. But don't expose your energy to them or be de-motivated because they don't believe in you. Make sure that throughout your journey you build up a fan base that believes in you and cheers you on.

Customers as a Resource

There is one other resource that many companies don't fully utilize for the information they can provide: *their customers.*

Your customers are as much your partners as your other resources. Treat them the same way you would treat a partner on the dance floor.

In ballroom performances, as my partner and I move together, I need to be completely present and alert to even subtle communications from him – slight movements in his hand or just his touch. Depending on what he is communicating physically, we could begin moving in circles, or we could be headed straight across the dance floor. I truly need to be aware of all his signals. It would show if I wasn't fully present.

You need to be THAT aware with your customers.

Your customers are communicating with you all the time. You can gain a lot of insight based on observing and gathering all the information you already have and putting it in front of you.

Customers can tell you what they want, what you should be thinking about in general, and also about trends in the marketplace. Any of these could open up new product or marketing ideas for you. They could say, for example, "Can you build me a mobile app that will make life convenient for me? I wish I had an app so I could process my payroll on the beach."

And like a genie in a bottle, you can grant them their wish.

Developing Customer Pattern Insights

Start by taking a look at your current list of clients or customers. Be aware and accepting of what the situation really is right now as you answer the following questions:

1. **Is there a commonality among your customers that you haven't noticed before?** Customer commonalities can tell you a lot about your marketing focus; who you might want to partner with for joint ventures; and what new products you could be developing based on their needs. For example, if you're an acupuncturist and a majority of your clients are women over the age of fifty, you could set up workshops and seminars geared specifically to the health needs of women of that age range. Again, at this stage, think only of the existing internal and external resources you have that you could utilize.

2. **What are customers really coming to you for?** Let go of your ideas about what you are promoting to them. Are you attuned to what they are asking you for?

3. **Are you, today, delivering to them what they're asking you for? Or are you trying to focus on marketing something new to them – like a particular product or service?** The market speaks to you. Your job is to listen. There are very few exceptions to this rule. You want to give your customers, as your partners, the respect that they deserve. You do that by delivering what they're asking for, whenever possible.

4. **Do you have a part of your package that will enable you to deliver what you need to deliver to the customer?** Question what you currently have available to you. Sometimes you already have something that is a small part of what you offer that can be expanded to satisfy a previously unheralded customer need.

Recently three customers from Fortune 5000 companies came and asked me to deliver workshops. Interestingly enough, they all wanted me to talk about the *same* topic! It was something I didn't offer yet.

The core business I'm promoting is assessment services. We assess where a company is by taking a full look at an organization, department, or division, in terms of the information they have right now. We then evaluate this information in terms of needs they may be concerned about in the future. For example, we show them how to expand to a new market. Thus, we might dive in and say, "Expanding to this particular market means you need to be certified and compliant. Here are the six things you need to do to execute this plan."

But these Fortune 5000 companies wanted us to perform a step before our assessment. Each of these organizations said, "Our leadership needs help with the decision-making process and communication of it before we address an assessment. Can you lead a workshop that can help?"

My audience was talking to me and telling me what they wanted instead of me trying to promote what I thought they wanted.

I needed to be aware and listening. Each of these clients had their own reasons for wanting the same thing.

Keep Building Customer Loyalty

There's one other item that needs to be mentioned about customers: You have to keep cultivating your relationship with them.

A lot of times in business, entrepreneurs get so excited or anxious about the future that they forget to listen to and take care of their current client base. They're so focused on "I want to attract new customers" that they overlook the customers they currently have and avoid viewing them as a partnership resource. Some business people practically ditch them, then they ask, "Why have my customers disappeared?"

Make sure to spend as much time on building customer loyalty as you do on attracting customers.

The Association Tango

Another external resource for businesses is associations. By that I mean chambers of commerce, networking events, nonprofit organizations, professional seminars, and other groups where you share common business development interest and can help each other with creativity, innovation, and growth. The type of environments you want to expose yourself to are ones where people authentically network and help each other thrive. Look for an association where the prevailing culture is about creating ideas and improvements.

The equivalents to associations in the dance world are the dance studios. Dancers want studios to positively challenge them and to help them grow and network. So dancers need to find places where people go, not to compete, but to work together to fulfill their dreams.

Whether you're a dancer or a business person, make sure you find groups that you click and resonate with.

Focus

If you've actually answered the questions in this chapter, you've come up with a lot of insight about a variety of areas in your business.

Don't try to handle everything at once.

Do what competitive dancers do; focus on one dance at a time. If you were to focus on the entire dance competition, particularly the 10-Dance, the thought of dancing from morning to night would distract and fatigue you. Focus your thoughts and your actions on one small aspect of the present, and you will create personal power.

Focusing is also the process of narrowing your concentration in order to eliminate specific unproductive or distracting occurrences. It is a method of fine-tuning your span of attention so that you stay in the moment, in the here and now.

If you give full attention to the present moment, you will find that you are energized and able to control the current reality. You must focus on the present in order to win.

Focus on what you want to achieve, not on what didn't work in the past. For example, a dancer could focus on a previous experience, perhaps one where she slipped, or on the future, such as upcoming problems she might encounter in the Rumba turn; either of these will only put pressure on her and impede her concentration on the next move, play, or dance she makes. The only way for her to make something positive happen is to focus on the present moment.

This is true in business as well. Get lost in the present. Become absorbed in your actions, oblivious to distractions around you.

Breathing and meditation techniques, like those mentioned previously, can train you to develop greater powers of attention by calming down distractions surrounding you. Not many can maintain this state for long periods of time, but you can provide yourself with the proper mental environment to develop your concentration skills rapidly. You can learn to discipline a wandering mind that diminishes your performance through distraction and diversion of energy.

Learn to recognize what makes your mind wander. When do you begin to think about stressors or distractions? Is it when you're at work? Or is it when you're among family and friends? Do you go inside yourself and obsess about how tired you are or about the error you just committed? Do you brood about an event in the past that didn't go exactly as you wanted it to or get anxious about an upcoming report that's due?

The past is not under your control; nor is the present or the future. When you focus your attention, only focus on what you can actually make an impact on. You can't control your competitors, or your teammates, or the weather, or the crowd (or even your mother). But you do have control over your own performance, attitude, engagement, energy level, and attentiveness. In dancing when you get wrapped up in the pressure of the things you can't control, dancing stops being fun.

The Right Map

Phew! We've covered a lot of ground, but trust me, insight is incredibly important. In order to make a plan of optimal actions, you need to have an accurate depiction of where you are. Imagine if you asked Siri (or Cortana or Peony or Google Now) how to get to the Statue of Liberty and she thought you were in Manhattan – but you actually were in Philadelphia. You would not get a direct and valid path to where you were going.

But you can take the optimal path when you start off knowing where you are. If you've answered the questions in this chapter, you now have the insight you need. This will help you create a plan of action that will bring you the opportunity to succeed in the best possible way. That is what you will work on in Chapter 3.

CHAPTER 3

CHOREOGRAPHY

Strategy Mapping Out What Your Story Is and Where You're Heading

Now that you've gained insight into where you are and what resources you have, it's time to map out where you are headed. In dance, this is where choreography comes in. Choreography is the mapping out of the steps, movements, and positions the dancers will take.

In the "Dance of the Business Mind," you choreograph the plan that will lead you to your transformation. You pick out the actual target you are aiming for.

My current dance partner, Genya Bartashevich, also my dance coach and choreographer, has been dancing since he was six. As a Professional-Amateur (Pro-Am) coach, Genya takes great pride in inspiring and helping his students achieve numerous titles including U.S. National, World Championship, and World Dance-Sport Series Championship.

"Before you make any decisions in choreography," Genya says, "you have to know what music you are using. Every dance has different musical structure and we have to use that musical pattern in order to look effective. Certain bars of the music are more powerful and it doesn't matter what track we're using as long as it's a real Cha Cha Cha, for example. It's always going to be the first bar, fifth, ninth, thirteenth, seventeenth, and so on. Always before I start the choreography, I make sure that my steps will meet a certain style of Cha Cha Cha and sync with the music we are using." [1]

---

1. Genya Bartashevich. Interview by author. Private lessons / recordings. Maryland, 2015-2016.

In business, you have to make sure that your "steps" (your business plan) match your "music" (your goal) as you forge ahead. As you create your map, go back to the insights you have gained, what resources you have, and crosscheck to make sure you are within your purpose and plan.

Efficiency and Effectiveness as Strategies

In business, part of ensuring your steps match your music is to seek balance between two different, yet related "routines." You can either choose to be more efficient with what you already have or you can be more effective by creating opportunities that don't exist.

When a business becomes more *efficient*, it's aiming to get the same or better results with a lower cost. You reduce what you spend on your workforce, suppliers, or your technology. Make sure you do this without affecting your mission, your daily operations, or even your work environment. When you prioritize efficiency, you are modifying past decisions to streamline what already exists. It's primarily an analytical approach.

According to Karina Smirnoff, *Dancing with the Stars* pro, and her professional dance partner Slavik Kryklyvyy, efficiency is key to the dance world. Karina says, "Technique is efficiency. Technique is important and is basic." Dancers are constantly referring back to their technique to improve and get better results. Slavik, who co-starred with Jennifer Lopez in the film *Shall We Dance?* adds that, "We go back to the technique to become better and improve. We want to chop out the unnecessary BS, unnecessary movement, and remove extra energy that is not necessary." [1]

Becoming more efficient is like taking a backwards step to lower costs, declutter, and fix a few things before you return to moving forward. "In dancing, [efficiency] is equivalent to going back to basics," says Genya. "In order to move forward, you have to take a step back and review basic actions, basic principles, and revisit before you can improve and go forward. You are taking a step back to become more efficient."

Karina Smirnoff and Slavik Kryklyvyy. Interview and notes by author. Private lessons / workshop / recordings. Virginia, 12/29/2015 - 01/01/2016.

What does *effectiveness* mean and how is it different? Effectiveness requires more of an emotional approach. There should be passion involved in whatever you're doing, just as there is in good dancing. "I always teach, as I was taught, that you have to create an emotion before the step. We call it 'creating a style,'" says Genya. "You have to be comfortable with emotion. It has to be true emotion – then no one will even remember what the step was if they feel what you feel. Some dancers are naturally expressive, so while we use that as a strength, we have to balance it with good technique. It creates a contrast."

Your goal in business, when you are creating something new, is to get your audience to feel what you feel. When you are being effective, you are creating something new that doesn't yet exist, so you are dealing with the future. When you seek to increase your effectiveness, you look at ways to expand your business, to develop innovative methods in your communications and collaboration, to add state-of-the-art functionality, and develop new ways to work with your workforce that inspire better habits and performance. You are striving to create a positive impact.

Sometimes it's as simple as creating a new product that propels you forward, such as going from a smartphone to a smartwatch, or adding innovative features, like adding sleep, heart rate, and blood pressure measurement to the Fitbit or Jawbone. Other times it's shifting your business to capitalize on a new market trend, like adding a mobile app – either producing one, using one, or both.

In a sense, aiming for effectiveness is like taking a step forward in dance, moving towards where you want to go, and shifting your weight. Slavik explains that being in alignment is crucial to propel yourself forward. "Imagine an athlete trying to make a big start to sprint...the foot, knee, hip joint, then back, should get one directional flow to be very effective....So to be more effective, all those joints have to align together to get an effective push. It's the same with dancing....In the Samba walk for example, it's very important to collect those joints together – knee, thigh, hip, and back."

In business, of course, you also have to focus on both ends of the equation to stay balanced. BIC®, the company that began with disposable pens, created part of their financial growth by becoming more efficient in producing ink, pencil leads, pen casings, etc. They became more effective by expanding their vision from one where they only produced writing equipment to the more general categories of school supplies and disposable products. School supplies allowed them to expand to items like glue sticks and pencil sharpeners. Their disposables, which are now ubiquitous, led them to find creative ways to provide consumers with throw-away lighters and razors.

Uber, at first blush, seems to be a predominantly effective business, focused on growth. They don't seem to be in the mode of reducing the cost of their workforce or consolidating their operations, yet. They are a young company, and it appears they are more interested in creating new jobs, greater safety for customers, enhanced technologies, and new territories. They have a powerful impact by creating better service for these new communities they will be working in.

But Uber's CEO, Travis Kalanick, understands that as the company ages, they will need to become more efficient. It is widely reported that Kalanick is betting on the creation of driverless vehicles – a move that is both efficient and effective. Recently, Uber poached forty researchers from Carnegie-Mellon's driverless car research program, and they've hired top people from Google's Maps division. Great maps are a critical component to driverless cars, and robots will definitely add more intelligence; thus the name artificial intelligence.

Efficiency is best viewed from a micro-level, with consolidation and cost reduction as short-term wins. Effectiveness requires more of a macro approach over a longer term. The impact is broader than just on your company; it also affects the marketplace and society at large. Also, effectiveness enhances your ability to adapt when changes take place in the environment.

The choreography of balancing efficiency and effectiveness can feel complex, but there are ways to make sure you stay focused on the right activities.

5 Steps to Help You Stay Balanced As You Dance Towards Transformation

#1 – Fresh Facts Will Increase Your Potential to Move Forward.

According to Isaac Asimov, the great and prolific writer of science-fiction, "Your assumptions are your windows on the world. Scrub them off every once in a while, or the light won't come in."

Genya says, "When a dancer achieves a certain title or a certain level, they often assume that position is now secure, and they don't look at things with a new perspective. That is when the chances are high for them to lose their title and position. But the ones who are achievers always keep working hard, use new approaches, use new sources, new styles, new ways – they don't assume that a past title is going to keep up with them and they are undefeatable."

As business owners and human beings, we tend to use the same old assumptions and data over and over again. It's easier, faster and doesn't tax our brain. But if you always use the same input, you'll always get the same output. So "scrub the windows" and grab some fresh information, maybe even from previously untapped sources. This will provide you a new angle from which to see things and help you find original approaches to make changes that will have a real impact. You want to find a balancing point between your old assumptions and your newer facts.

REAL WORLD EXAMPLE: Most businesses review their annual sales figures the same exact way year after year, using worn out information and assumptions. If you are in a transformational mode, the way you looked at and measured things in the past needs to be integrated with new lenses, like the latest technologies, new demographic groups, additional products, current trends, or just a fresh pair of eyes to shake your business up.

#2 – Walk the Line Between Constructive Criticism and Perfectionism.

In dance, when all your weight is on one leg and the other leg is up in the air, it's easy to topple over. In business, if you focus too heavily on others' constructive criticism, you can easily fall victim to perfectionism and self-doubt. This can freeze you up and halt your progress.

Criticism requires balance. When you are the one observing others with a critical eye, you don't want be too harsh. Yet you need to continually look diligently at how your business can be improved. Constructive criticism can lead to the positive changes that maximize our achievement. Sometimes people can be sensitive to suggestions for change, especially if your company has been doing the same thing the same way for a long time. It might help to hire an outside consultant to assess, evaluate, and make suggestions for improvements to your business model, as well as your people and processes. Make sure you hire someone who can see what needs to be fixed without being too negative.

REAL WORLD EXAMPLE: Recently my company was soliciting bids from various outside accounting vendors. As we were evaluating options, we noticed major differences in how two companies were trying to win our business. Vendor A went to great lengths to evaluate our records and point out itty bitty flaws while making them sound grand. They complained about how difficult and time consuming the work would be and didn't give us a firm price or timeline. Vendor B said they understood where we were coming from and that the work wouldn't be a problem. They assured us that they deal with businesses with complex processes such as ours all the time, and gave us a quote for a fixed rate.

You can guess who we went with, right? We did hear Vendor A's constructive criticism, but we also realized that we didn't need to overcomplicate things.

#3 – Interact with Your Surroundings Instead of Tuning Them Out.

Some dancers enter their own world when they're dancing, as if the audience is not there. Better dancers perform in a way that the audience feels included.

In business, tune into partners, clients, and co-workers instead of viewing them as distractions. What feels like an interruption could lead to your next big breakthrough. And while you're paying attention to others, don't forget to pay attention to your own gut instinct. There are enough neurons in your gut to create the equivalent of a second brain, yet many people ignore this intuitive sense to their own detriment.

In business, listen to your audience (i.e., market) as well. Often this takes place in social media, which can help you discover market trends and important information about how people feel about your company, products, and services (or even how they feel about your competitor's offerings). When people tell you what they want, listen! #1 *New York Times* bestselling author, Harvey Mackay, writes that, "You learn when you listen. You earn when you listen – not just money, but respect."

REAL WORLD EXAMPLE: My company, which has primarily provided software and services directly to the federal government for the past 25 years, learned through social connections and engagements that technology manufacturers mostly needed our help to give them traction in the government space. Though this varied from our traditional services, we paid attention, and added a new program to meet these needs. Now we also act as a distributor, help with partner engagement, capture market intelligence, create content messaging, foster business development, and provide support in the areas of document management, proposal writing and contracts, certification and compliance. In today's world, you have to become aware of the messages your audiences are sending you about their desires and needs, not just what you think will be of most benefit to your company. Then determine if you can modify your business model to fulfill them and if it fits within your company culture to do so.

#4 – Optimize Your Energy – Exceeding Expectations vs. Over-Delivery.

In dancing there are rules, and even a rulebook. There is a minimum standard that must be met to place in a competition. You would think that, in order to win, a dancer would try to perform the most difficult or complicated routine. However, great dancers exceed expectations, yet stay within the boundaries of the rulebook. Over-delivering and performing far outside of expectations can actually disqualify a dancer. Even though it might look beautiful, certain activities are not within the scope of the competition. There are some dancers that enter at, say, the bronze level, but try to turn in a silver or gold level performance. They wind up performing choreography that is outside the proscribed boundaries and are often disqualified.

Genya has a great example of this. "I once did an experiment," he says, where I asked one of my students who just finished learning silver level choreography to compete in a higher level – open gold division. Imagine the surprise when the least experienced dancer on the floor with choreography two levels down from everybody else finished second in the whole competition. This was possible because we weren't trying to over-deliver with the 'tricks,' but rather, to exceed expectations thanks to her technical skill." The moral of the story, he says, is to "focus on your technique and really master your skills, rather than trying to impress judges by adding difficulty to your choreography."

One parallel to this in business has to do with customer service. Sometimes it can be a struggle to balance meeting a customer's expectations and staying within the original expectations for a project's scope. There are situations when giving the customer significantly more than you promised, or over-delivering, may be a detriment to your overall relationship.

Let's say you are tasked to deliver a report, but the way you deliver it exceeds customer expectations. Maybe you used a new collaborative tool or utilized fresh visual images and diagrams. Over-delivery is to deliver outside the scope of what is expected. You were assigned to gather intelligence and provide a certain assessment, but rather, you forged ahead and executed based on your findings, hoping the customer would be happy. But instead, you may have veered from the original mission or established a dangerous pattern of providing free services.

REAL WORLD EXAMPLE: An ongoing steady decrease in customer traffic by a relatively small shipping store in a community with a tiny population was mistakenly attributed to weak customer service. This organization tried to fix what they saw as the problem by giving customers excessive attention, lower rates for their regular services, and creating a policy that reasonable requests would never be turned down. Customers enjoyed the changes, but sales remained flat and costs increased considerably. In this case, over-delivery beyond the ordinary scope of business had a negative effect. Instead of uncovering the root cause of the traffic decline by looking for fresh facts, this organization acted too fast, using old assumptions. The problem wasn't their customer service, but rather falling behind with the outside advances in technology, including mobile apps that made some of their normal offerings obsolete.

#5 – Focus on Yourself to Better Focus on Your Partner (Customer).

Oliver Cromwell, a 17th century English military and political leader, said once that, "He who stops being better stops being good."

In dance, you have to maintain a balance between your focus on yourself and your focus on your partner. "To focus on yourself helps to show yourself as an independent character. When dancing with a partner, you must have a very clear understanding of your role, otherwise it becomes difficult to communicate," says Genya. "Sometimes, you need to discuss what that choreography means to each of you, so you can show it in uniquely personal ways. For example, as my partner, Yana Mazhnikova, and I were preparing for World Latin Showdance Championships, we decided that we were going to dance a piece that we had practiced for years and could perform in our sleep. Throughout, we each assumed that each of us understood the story the same way, but in our own minds, each of us had a different version of the story. Be very specific with your partner and don't assume he or she is thinking what you are thinking – communicate and re-communicate. But not to the point where it becomes draining."

Balance the focus given to your own story and that of your partner, and make sure you are in alignment. Keep in mind that it is okay to take a break and work on your own self, your own techniques, and your own beauty, so that when you are working with your partner, you are stronger and sharper, together. Otherwise, your partner may grow while you remain stagnant, which could eventually create a gap between your abilities and theirs that becomes an issue.

In business, sometimes we spend so much time helping our clients optimize their products or services that we neglect our own business. We miss opportunities for growth and even neglect our own company or personal morale. It may seem difficult, but it's essential to continue the process of internal growth while you also pay great attention to your customers. Continue to improve everything that has to do with your company, starting with yourself. Also, look for ways that you can transform your products, your relationship with your partners, and your team.

REAL WORLD EXAMPLE: To be honest, this last item can be a struggle for me. As a business owner, I give a lot of attention to my key clients and play a variety of roles for each of them. But, I've found that it's essential to balance my focus between their business and my own. H. Jackson Brown, Jr., author of *Life's Little Instruction Book*, says, "Talent without discipline is like an octopus on roller skates. There's plenty of movement, but you never know if it's going to be forward, backwards, or sideways." I make an extra effort to make sure my team and I have weekly meetings where we brainstorm possibilities for improvement and growth and then follow-up by actually working on making these internal and external transformations. This energizes all of us, which ultimately helps us perform better for our customers.

Create Opportunities by Remaining Aware

As you journey through the four phases – the decision to transform, gather insight, create a strategy and execute your performance – it is important that you are mentally aware of your progress throughout each of these processes.

Once you initiate the first phase, you become mindful of activities you need to act on or change. After the insight phase, you're aware of what you need to collect in terms of data, information, and resources. You get to a point where you're aware of being aware; this means you know what you're looking for and want to accomplish. You are constantly attuned to your surroundings, and like a hunter, some barely conscious part of you is looking for tracks on the ground that will lead you to your prey.

Your awareness widens to include opportunities to move in the right direction that you wouldn't ordinarily pick up on. These are not pipeline opportunities, by which I mean potential clients, but rather new ways to plan more strategically.

I work with a lot of lawyers. I help plan, design, and integrate technology usage into their practices that greatly impacts their people and processes. I see how important awareness is to the litigation process, especially in the discovery stage. Just like on TV, lawyers must be aware of all testimony and evidence that might improve their case.

What frustrates many lawyers about their paralegals is that they don't pick up on opportunities to look more closely at something that, with deeper investigation, could move the needle. Usually paralegals spend a ton of time going through documents saying, "We're aware of these documents, and they look pretty much the same as what we've already reviewed." But that's not the point; they're supposed to look for new information or a pattern of behavior. Even the slightest detail could lead to a breakthrough in a case.

Awareness of awareness is like being a poker player who searches for tells – facial expressions or movements that are giveaways as to whether a competitor has a good hand or is bluffing. The idea is to be fully alert and on top of your game, with a heightened sense of openness to whatever patterns shows up. Your attitude should be one of, "I don't know exactly what I'm looking for, but I'll know it when I see it."

Bring that attitude to bear when you are mapping out a strategic plan. By being receptive, you will find information and ideas that support your ideas and path.

Connect With Your Goals

Goals are dreams or mental images you choose to work towards. When you are not connected with your goals, you may feel indecision, conflict, or dissatisfaction. When you are connected with your goals you act with a sense of self-confidence and well-being.

Feeling confident that you can achieve your goal helps enhance your feeling of connectedness. To achieve that confidence, seek and highlight what you are already good at, and apply these strengths in other areas, so you can expedite overall progress towards your goal. When Genya starts to choreograph for a student that he is dancing with, he starts by figuring out what they already do well. "If the student looks good doing one version of, let's say, a lock-step, then I make sure that choreography for competition includes different variations of that lock-step," he says, "because I already know they look good doing that. So no matter when the judge is evaluating us as a dance couple, we're going to look effective dancing together. We're going to look good."

He says that students may make the mistake of planning routines by emulating others instead of reflecting on their own unique talents. They fail to realize that it has taken others significant time and effort to make their performances look easy. "A lot of times, we see something that the champions are doing and people come in and they are like, 'I want to do that.' But the student doesn't really realize that it might take 10 or even 15 years to perfect that look, yet they want it today. In the end, they're never satisfied with it because it doesn't look good on them. It's important that you have your own style and the teacher must create a style for the dancer, so then the choreography looks organic with the person that is doing it. We have to make sure that technically it's done properly, on the best level that that dancer can achieve in the moment."

As I'm writing this, I have a performance coming up soon that I'm really excited about. Right now, we are choreographing my Paso Doble and my Samba mix to a Cirque du Soleil song. I am truly creating my own style, my own character. Of all the ones I've performed, this may be the one that most expresses my personality and voice.

In business, you have to do the same thing; use your own voice as part of mapping out your strategy. Our dreams and visions are unified with our actions and behavior through the process of setting goals that are both challenging and realistic. One way to achieve big dreams is to create a combination of both short-term and long-term goals. Short-term goals need to be realistic and attainable. For example, if you want to start running, you don't aim for a marathon right away. You can have that in the back of your mind, but you have to start off with what you can do without injuring yourself, even if you only start with a quarter of a mile. You will eventually have the stamina to increase that distance little by little.

Make sure you celebrate all of your milestones. Your first mile run will be a terrific accomplishment. Eventually, you can achieve the thirteen miles that mark a half-marathon. Don't be unrealistic with your timeline, otherwise you will become disillusioned. Realistic, achievable goals help build confidence and keep you motivated and enthusiastic, lessening your fear of overwhelming long-term goals.

My long-term goal of winning at an open gold level dance competition enables me to experience a wonderful process and journey – to be on track with the joy and fulfillment I felt as I first entered bronze, and now silver competitions. Reaching the initial milestones of winning at these lower levels have provided the encouragement that I might be able to achieve my ultimate desire. But, I am not overly attached to my long-term goal. If I create anxiety and pressure for both myself and my partner to get to win first place in the open gold level, then I am not enjoying the journey.

My interim goals allow me to evaluate my performance at each step on the way to the bigger, major goals. For example, I need to compete in several more dance competitions, a short-term goal, to get to a level where I can compete at the open gold level. This allows the process to remain challenging and keeps my connection with my ultimate goal strong. If along the way my goal changes, then I need to be flexible enough to let it change.

Definitions

One thing that's incredibly important in dance is for the choreographer and dancers to use the same words to describe the movements that are to be made. Dance is full of its own vocabulary.

For example, some define and explain the term *weight transfer* differently. Genya explains, "One coach might mean to shift the weight fully in one action; another coach might indicate to split the weight between the two legs and then transfer the weight."

While many refer to a weight change as shifting from one leg to the other in a delayed walk demonstration, Slavik defines it as the transfer of weight within the same standing leg – moving from the heel, to the ball of the foot, to the toes.

Even the simple word *balance* can imply different meanings based on how it is used. "In dance, we use the terms in-balance, off-balance, and out-of-balance," explains Genya. "In-balance means you control your own balance. Most likely you will be vertical, engaging your core, having proper posture. Off-balance is when you don't appear to be balanced, but you can still maintain, regain, and control your balance. Out-of-balance is when you need the support of your partner. You cannot do it on your own."

As you can see, choreographers and their dancers have to understand each other completely. A misunderstanding during a dance like the Argentinian Tango, with its lovely leg flicks, could result in the man being kicked in their private parts! Even worse, someone could fall and get seriously injured. Everyone has to take the time to make sure that all parties are on the same page and each person understands exactly what the other means.

Confusion over the simplest of wording, surprisingly enough, can wreak havoc in business. I've seen negative outcomes in various organizations due to miscommunication, where one person thought a common phrase meant one thing and someone else interpreted it as meaning another.

Here's a simple example: One time I was going through some tedious documentation with a colleague. We were reading it line by line. I would say, "continue" to her, as in "it's repetitive, let's skip to the next part," and she would think I meant it was a "continuation" of the document. Little words can have a big impact. You have to share the same definitions and make an effort at the beginning of any project to be conscious of this. Whoever is leading the project should always start by defining all terms so that everyone uses the same definition for everything.

That's why many companies use visual techniques to avoid communication misinterpretations.

Illusions

A dance performance is filled with illusions. One such example is the spins that dancers perform. Some spins look very fast, but they are not as fast as they appear. The way these spins are crafted, particularly the stop, creates the illusion of speed. From the standpoint of the audience, it looks fast – but the extent of the speed is just a trick.

There are many opportunities to create positive illusions in performances. Karina jokingly says, "People come up and say 'oh my gosh you're so much smaller in person than I thought.' That's a good thing. You want to look a lot taller than you actually are when you dance."

Have you noticed that when you are looking at a distant object with your eyes and looking at the same object from the same distance through the camera lens of your smartphone, the view from the camera lens appears to be zoomed in – even though it is from the same distance? Why is the view from the camera lens different from that of the human eye?

Most people believe that video is an extremely accurate depiction of what is being filmed, but that's an illusion. Check it out. Watch a performance of something while you record it – then watch the video. They are different.

Your eyes move at a different speed than your smartphone's video camera. Why is that? Without getting into too much detail, a camera's movement doesn't capture images as consistently and with the same speed as the human eye. Your brain perceives continuous motion, whereas the video captures motion in a series of snapshot frames and then pieces them together. This results in a significant difference between the two.

Illusions are sometimes present in business when it comes to interpretation and analysis of data. Just like with video, we think we are looking at an accurate depiction of reality, when in fact, things are not as clear as we think. For example, someone might be choreographing the situation in a way that misdirects our attention and alters our perceptions, so that we misinterpret the "facts" that we see.

It's a lot like what happens when we witness a magician use a handsaw to "cut" his female assistant in half. Our eyes see one thing, but our mind believes another. When what we see doesn't fit our expectations of reality, our minds then search for a logical explanation.

Have you ever seen this magic trick? What was your reaction? It was probably, "That's impossible, it can't be!" You then probably explained it away, saying, "That must've been a trick cabinet," or "There were two assistants as part of that illusion!"

Your inability to explain with certainty what happened wasn't because you weren't paying enough attention to the trick; it was due to the magician distracting you, taking your focus away from the actions that would tip you off to the trick, and placing it onto something inconsequential.

This can happen in business as well. We focus on the wrong data and let it distract us from what's really going on. This is particularly true with visual data.

Our perception of data varies based on how they are presented through graphs and charts. Understanding how this happens can help us change our analysis and improve the way we make decisions.

How Your Mind Works When Presented with Visual Data

Visuals are increasingly used to share ideas, content, and information in a bite-sized manner, catering to short attention spans and busy schedules. Not only are visuals used in newspapers, commercials, and 24-hour news channels to influence audiences, but they're also more widely used in corporate environments to quickly review, collaborate, and make strategic decisions using information, data and applications. They are used so frequently that the sheer volume can be overwhelming, potentially leading to flawed decision making.

When we encounter cleverly designed visual data, such as engaging infographics, we experience a myriad of reactions and responses. When you see something intriguing, your visual cortex offers up a lightning fast perception of what you just saw. However, the process of interpretation does not stop there. What you saw and – note here – "paid attention to" then travels to the cerebral cortex. This is where the actual cognitive, conscious thinking analysis occurs and is then stored in your memory.

We Experience (Perspective)
Thus We Interpret (Perception)

For our purposes, perception is the brain's starting point to receive, understand, and process sensory information.

As humans we draw upon our perspective, as formed from prior experiences, when perceiving new data and information. We make predictions of what will/should happen next based on our histories. But, is the current situation truly like those of the past? Are you perceiving and interpreting visual information through a clouded lens or a clear one? The more embedded our beliefs, the more difficult it is for us to see anything in a truly different way. Perspective is tough to change, and is consistently reinforced by our perceptions.

Seeing Things the Way They Really Are Is a Challenge

Imagine you see an eye-catching infographic in the local newspaper. This particular image is meant to influence the reader to believe that widget prices are rising too quickly, as demonstrated by a graph on an x and y axis. However, and this happens frequently, there is a break on the y axis, making the increase look more substantial. The average reader will not notice that and instead will be influenced by the inaccurate message that the image conveys.

By focusing on your perception, or how you interpret data, you can improve the solidity of your overall perspective, in other words, the evaluation of the data. By questioning what you perceive, you can adopt a flexible, fluid, open-minded perspective.

Here's what to look for:

1. Ask yourself if your interpretations are based on past experiences. Start by honing in on what your past experiences are. For example, when you read sales documents for a product heralding its many benefits, are you influenced by a general affinity for the brand? Do you really believe the validity of the product benefits, or do you just love the brand? Pay attention to your perspective, which is the way

you evaluate information and how you arrive at your conclusion (your perception). Are you seeing the forest for the trees? This is how to start noticing and recognizing patterns of behavior and become aware of what's actually true in the present.

2. Evaluate if the current situation is truly the same as the past. What is different? Perhaps, in terms of the example above, you realize that your positive association is based on a different product that is no longer made by this company and does not have significant bearing on your current decision.

3. After thinking about it this way, what are your perceptions about the situation now? Did you change your mind, or would you like to stay on course?

If you have a team, observe your team's dynamics and interaction with visual data. What are their perspectives and perceptions? It is important to help them understand these issues as well. The key here is to welcome a non-judgmental view in order to be open to new information and make impactful decisions.

See Through Sleight of Hand

What you **believe** you see is what cements your perspective. If you don't challenge yourself to ask how the magician does his illusion, you'll never learn new tricks. There are many ways of interpreting events, each of which leads to different conclusions. This is why you must constantly question visuals, no matter how pretty they are. You must stay attuned to and aware of who the choreographer is and what illusions they are employing to make scenarios appear a certain way. And when you are working with a team, be mindful of each other's perspectives and perceptions and how they affect decisions.

Our perception of reality is what governs the perspective direction of our decisions. Make sure yours is based on the present so you can redefine the future instead of being stuck on a treadmill in the past.

Marketing Your Story

In the Paso Doble I'm currently working on, the bullfight dance, where I, the female dancer, play different roles at various times; shifting from representing a flamenco gypsy dancer to a cape and then to a bull. (Some dance professionals insist that the female must never become the bull!)

Towards the end of my story, I die while in the character of the bull. Since it's a dance, I have to communicate each of these roles to the audience through my actions, without words. They need to be able to see all of the aspects of the Spanish bullfight and be able to tell when I am the cape, the flamenco gypsy dancer, and the bull. They also have to understand that I've actually died at the end of my piece. So my choreographer and I worked hard to make this communication extremely clear and understandable.

The same thing happens in business. You need everyone you communicate with to be in alignment with the story you are creating, including those within your company, your partners, and, of course, your customers. Look closely to see if everyone is able to follow your story, or whether there is a key ingredient that's just in your head and hasn't been shared.

If I'm dancing and doing a choreographed piece, the audience becomes a part of that story. They embrace the story and merge it to theirs. In business, you hope to craft a story that people relate to, where they say to themselves, "Oh yeah, I get it, I understand, that makes sense to me." But sometimes it doesn't.

That's what happened when Coca-Cola came out with New Coke in 1985. It was one of the biggest failures to communicate a story properly in the modern business era. Coca-Cola didn't do a good job of letting people know they were planning a new version of their signature soda; they let the media know they were making a big announcement just four days before they unveiled the new product. They also never let consumers in on *why* they were doing it. They just went ahead and launched a new flavor that completely replaced the old flavor. They had no understanding that customers had an emotional connection to the original formula and wouldn't buy into the idea of a new version. Coca-Cola was clearly telling the wrong story – so much so that protest groups were formed, and after 77 days, Classic Coke came back as an alternative to New Coke. Ultimately, New Coke was discontinued, first in the United States, and then worldwide in 2002.

The decision to create New Coke came from the corporate office, primarily to try to stave off competition from Pepsi. It's a prime example of having a story in your head that no one else understands.

Apple, on the other hand, found a way to communicate the right story when they released the iPod. They started with a vision of how consumers could use music in the technology miniaturization era where it was possible to download files from the Internet. That was their internal story. That story turned out to be spot on.

It also fit what was becoming their branding. As Walter Isaacson writes in the biography, *Steve Jobs*, " . . . the iPod became the essence of everything Apple was destined to be: poetry connected to engineering, arts and creativity intersecting with technology, design that's bold and simple." [1]

Externally, though, it took a couple of tries to get their story right. Their first commercial, released in 2001, shows a man dancing in his chair to music on his computer. He then downloads the song he's listening to onto his iPod, closes his laptop, puts his earbuds in, and starts dancing around the room. The ad ends with him sticking his iPod in his jacket pocket, and leaving his home, followed by a voiceover that says: "iPod: a thousand songs in your pocket."

According to Apple's creative director, Ken Segall, author of *Insanely Simple: The Obsession that Drives Apple's Success*, using a real person was the downfall of the ad. Though some people may have found the dancing man cool, others thought he was too geeky. Some people on the Internet were derisively calling the ad a commercial for the "iClod." [2]

The other problem was that the story didn't matter to Windows users, as the iPod at that point was only compatible with the Mac.

In 2003, however, Apple found a way to tell the iPod tale that not only connected with consumers, but also became an advertising classic. Their secret was to simplify the story they told, include two or more people, turn them into dancing silhouettes, and have them move to really cool, energetic music. In short, they captured the *emotion* of what it meant to have an iPod in your life.

1. Isaacson, Walter. *Steve Jobs*. New York: Simon & Schuster, 2011.
2. Lucas NM, "10 Shocking Facts About The Most Successful Ad Campaigns," *The Richest*, June 30, 2015, http://www.therichest.com/rich-list/most-shocking/10-shocking-facts-about-the-most-successful-ad-campaigns/

In the first version of the commercial, each silhouette danced against its own single background color – electric blue, golden yellow, and lime green. The only other color in the ad was the white of the iPod and its earbuds. The wires to the dancers' ears danced along with them. The white brilliantly contrasted with the two other colors it was displayed with.

The TV commercial told the story so well, and so memorably, that Apple was able to use stills of the silhouetted images in billboard and bus stop advertisements.

This iPod campaign gave the entire Apple brand a patina of fun. It made Apple seem so cool that Steve Jobs realized that it would positively impact their iMac computer sales enough so that he moved $75 million from the iMac advertising budget to the iPod campaign, believing that iMac sales would thrive due to an overall increase in the love for all things Apple inspired by this commercial. In other words, he took the approach that a rising tide lifts all boats. This allowed Apple to spend one hundred times what their competitors were spending on portable music players, leaving the iPod unrivaled in their market.

Just as important, the story told in this advertising created an emotional connection to the Apple brand with regard to portables, which aided future products like the iPhone and the iPad.

Creating a Character or Persona That Connects to the Audience

There are very specific ways in which an emotional connection can be made between the dancer and the audience.

Genya choreographs dancers so that connection begins as they walk on stage. "It has to start emotionally," he says. "When I choreograph somebody, I want to make sure that before the music starts . . . we understand what the character of the dancer is, without a sound. That means that your body has a certain shape, it has a certain mood, it has a beginning of a story or if you are in the middle of the story that means you start with a different emotional stage."

He starts with where they are positioned on the dance floor.

"When somebody comes in and I need to create a new choreography, I visualize that person, I visualize the person that she's dancing with and I already have a starting point, how they're going to start moving, which place in the ballroom is going to be the most effective, why we're going to start moving either next to each other, or in front of each other. I get a mental snapshot of the way the dance is going to flow, and then I incorporate steps into the timing or I create timing into the steps; in other words, I start creating a rhythm that needs to exist between two people."

In business, you need to create that same impact within the marketplace. Make sure that your business has its own unique style, its own personality that shines. You need to find out what your voice is within your business; don't just replicate somebody else – create and own a distinct personality. Sometimes in business we call that your unique value proposition, which conveys how your business differs from that of your competitors. This will help your business connect emotionally to its audience.

Your distinct personality also helps to make bold choices in both business and dance.

Genya says boldness comes from taking risks. "Sometimes to stand out, you have to do something different," he explains. "The hardest thing is to create your own style and understand what it is and stay true to it."

He says the trick is to make decisions that you might not ordinarily make or might not have made a year ago. Trust your instincts. "If I want to do Tango in the middle of Rumba and I think it looks sexy, I'm going to do Tango in the middle of Rumba. People reacted to it when they saw it for the first time and indicated that it was different. It was a bold decision. I think making those decisions will make you stand out."

Bold decisions are what turned Richard Branson into a billionaire. Once known primarily as the owner of Virgin Records, which started out as a chain of record stores, he made a bold move to create a record label with his own artists. Even bolder was his decision to buy a Jumbo Jet and create Virgin Atlantic Airlines with that one 747. (He also boldly negotiated with Boeing to be able to return the plane within a year if his airline didn't work out.) He is now the chairman of the Virgin Group, which runs over 400 companies.

Creating Bold Decisions for Your Business

Here's a way to come up with bold strategies: Ask yourself, "What's the farthest I can go with this?" Don't limit yourself or worry if the ideas you come up with are unreachable, undoable, or completely unrealistic. Just use them as points of departure. You can always reign them in and make them practical later. But if you start off with extreme ideas, what you wind up with may turn out to be bolder than what you originally had in mind.

For example, if you are opening a new restaurant, you might think about giving away free meals for a week as a way to get people to show up and spread word of mouth. Or you might decide that's not practical and offer free desserts for the first week.

One word of caution, though: Don't be too bold when it comes to safety. Back in the 1970s, Domino's Pizza used to offer the extremely bold pizza delivery guarantee, "30 minutes or it's free." But after losing several multi-million dollar lawsuits for accidents caused by their drivers running red lights, they removed that guarantee and offered to refund your money or remake your pizza if you're dissatisfied.

A Little Contrast is Necessary

As spectators, we all love the exciting moments in dance. A high leap, an extended set of turns, or a series of fast, powerful lifts and dips can create a climax that at times is unforgettable. But a dance can't be made only of climaxes; it would be exhausting for the dancers, and believe it or not, it would be boring for the audience.

Why? We have an innate need for contrast.

The Paso Doble I'm working on has moments of high energy, but it also has moments of complete stillness that allow the drama to sink in. Sometimes it's slow and builds, and other times it goes from fast to slow controlled movement, such as when as the bull, I attack my partner, the matador, and he stabs me as I slowly die.

In business, you need to create drama as well. If you're bringing something to market, there's that drama that something is coming up, something is coming out, but we're not going to tell you what that is until something happens.

Apple is very good at enticing you about what's coming out next.

Creating anticipation isn't just good for the external marketplace; it's good for your internal employees as well. That's what stirs up creativity and innovation. Some people think of drama as being bad, but often, it can also be good. Aspects of negative drama can also stir up some interesting thoughts and creativity.

There's also another level to consider. In dance, you can't constantly think about the technique and how you're going to change or improve. Sometimes, you just need to focus on enjoying the process. "When you stop enjoying it, it means you are diving into too much detail and losing creativity and passion," says Genya. "There are things that are necessary like working on technique, musicality, and beauty – but passion helps you drive through difficult moments or moments that you don't enjoy as much."

There are other times, however, that you need to push yourself or push your partner. Or you even need to push your client.

Sometimes in business you move quickly in order to meet a deadline. There are also phases where you move slowly as you incubate an idea. Many times you go through test runs, where you have consumers do a trial test, also known as a beta test. With products, there is a lot of beta testing, followed by focus groups where users talk about their experience with the item or service that they used. Registering that feedback can be a slow time, where you absorb what has been said, then make incremental improvements to your original product. But these times can be extremely fruitful. So as in a beautiful dance, make sure your business has both climaxes and slow times.

Take a Step Back to Move Forward

Vibeke Toft, head of the World Dance Council (WDC) Education Department, says, "As a dancer, when you think of choreography, your mind becomes organized. When your mind is organized, you become focused on every single moment. When you're so focused on every single moment, your brain becomes occupied. When your brain becomes occupied, you're not free to feel."

In business, this means you need to delegate. If you hold on to every detail, it's like a dancer who focuses on every single moment. Not only will this slow your progress down to a crawl, it will also make you unable to see your work clearly. When you delegate something, you can review the work of the person who did it with fresh eyes and see if there's anything that needs changing. When you do all the work yourself, you are too close to it to understand what might need improving. You feel overwhelmed and your life can often seem completely unbalanced by all the work you're doing.

If you delegate, however, you have room to breathe, and your choreography gets finished more quickly, elegantly, and efficiently.

Once it's finished, you're ready to take the next step.

After You Complete Your Choreography

Before you move on, take a moment to celebrate the accomplishment of another milestone on the way towards transforming your business.

You're now at a point where you have your next moves mapped out, and you have the tools in place to make those moves. You've got a strategy. You're actually ready to expand into a new market – or execute other plans you might have. You've prepared yourself and your team to take the next step and find the "props" and "costumes" you'll need to help you with your "performance."

In the dance world, this stage of gathering costumes and props will help with the strategy of when, where, and how to use them. It can be that way in the business world as well. In Chapter 4, I'll show you what you need to think about as you practice, rehearse, and then execute your strategy.

CHAPTER 4

PRACTICE AND REHEARSAL

Strategy Execution

With our choreography complete and our strategy mapped, it's time to practice and rehearse. There's a lot of mental and physical preparation that goes with this stage. It also requires persistence and drive. Visualization is another helpful strategy to achieve something that's as close to perfection as you are presently capable of. Nobody's perfect, so practice doesn't make perfect. It just increases the odds that you will do the absolute best you can do when it comes time to perform.

The business equivalent to practicing and rehearsing is strategy execution. It takes place right before your launch. Your launch, of course, is the equivalent to a performance. Typically, this phase has to do with reporting. For example, if you're doing a software execution, you're going to go through a testing phase before you actually launch the software application. This doesn't just apply to software. Whatever you're launching, you're going to need to go through a beta phase, which means internal testing, before you bring it to full-blown production.

For example, with Uber's driverless cars, reaching the point of having testers ride in the car is the equivalent of practicing and rehearsing. The development of the intelligence to drive the car – the creation of the software and mechanical interfaces that led to them being able to enter this test phase – is the equivalent to choreography. Now they can measure their efficiency and effectiveness. They are getting feedback before they launch this product to the public. In this particular case, there may be government regulations to deal with before they launch, but that's not the norm for most new product launches.

Nonetheless, in terms of the development process, Uber is executing their strategy and going back to the drawing board as things need to be improved.

This happens everywhere, no matter what you're creating, whether it be a product or a service. It's true in the dance world as well, where you are constantly improving.

In my own dance performance of the Paso Doble with the Cirque du Soleil song, we kept improving what we were doing right up until the day before the performance, even though this was a showcase and not a competition. There were some movements that seemed off. The transition from one movement to another just didn't feel right. It wasn't coordinated and the connection wasn't there. In order for us to communicate better, we had to tweak some things. We had to say, "Okay, is this movement efficient?" We made sure to focus on the important parts and alter the remaining ones. In our choreography, rhythm was the most important factor. So we changed other aspects of the performance while keeping the rhythm intact. When you choreograph, you either do it around the music, around certain steps, or around the character. It's up to you to figure out what is working and what isn't.

We also needed to make sure our changes would be effective. Would these new movements be as powerful as the previous ones and would they portray what we wanted them to portray?

Strategy and execution come into play during practice and rehearsal for dance, for products and services, or whatever else you have going on. It's something you must do before you launch anything. You don't want to have to recall a product or rework services. These fix-it-afterwards scenarios are way more expensive than simply getting things right before you launch. That's why this chapter is very important. Make sure you constantly test your performance before you move forward.

Writing this book has involved constant tweaking, and I've had lots of eyes on it. I am calling this review and edit, but it is really constant modification, just like a test phase. When we edit chapters, instead of feeling like I'm moving backwards, I feel like I'm progressing forward. If I make tweaks in my dancing, I'm making positive advancements with movements that feel right. If Uber gets feedback from their testing staff or the riders in their driverless cars, they're evolving to become better and better.

Three Questions to Discuss with Your Partner

As you begin this phase, make sure you and your partner or team are in sync about what you want to accomplish and how. Here are three things to think about:

1. **What are your rehearsal parameters and definitions?** Though we mentioned definitions in the last chapter, this is a different stage of the conversation. You want to talk about what your definition of success is, as well as what your timing, deadlines, and goals are both in terms of overall rehearsal/execution and on a more near-term basis. Karina Smirnoff of *Dancing with the Stars* says, "You both have to have equal amount of dedication and work ethic or workaholic nature."

2. **What do you have in common?** It's good to make a conscious effort to become aware of this as soon as you can. On the one hand, it's a nice way to get started on the right foot, with something you can easily get into together. On the other hand, rehearsal and execution can both cause moments of conflict and tension. One way to break the tension is go back and work on something easy and more fun, where you both have the same strengths.

   In dance, you both might share a common way of connecting to the musicality of the piece you're working on, even if one of you is more technically proficient and the other is a better performer.

   In business, you and your partner may have different skill sets; perhaps one of you is more of an idea person and the other is good at finding the holes in ideas. But you both may share a love of being the first one on your block to have the latest technology.

3. **What is the grandest vision of what you're trying to accomplish?** A big success requires a big dream. In dance, how far would you like to take what you're working on? Do you want to compete at a gold level, or merely perform in a showcase? In business, what opportunities are out there that you can capitalize on? How enormous do you want your market to get? You never know where dreaming can take you, so make sure you include it as part of your process. Also, when the days get

long and there's been more perspiration than inspiration, these are the thoughts that can sustain you and give you an extra burst of energy.

Karina says that if you have the same goal, you both will work towards that goal. "If people are not in-sync with where they want to end up," she says, "the partnership will not work. In Russia there is a painting and a poem where there are a swan, a pike, and a crawfish pulling things in different directions. For business and for partnership this is the worst thing you can do. You can have different elements, but people should be pulling in the same direction."

A "test" partnership should also be done sometimes, before entering into a fully blown-out, long-term business partnership. Test to see if both companies can work together and if the cultures of the companies are in sync. Go through one pilot deal together and determine how good of a fit the relationship is and work through some of the processes and logistics.

Use Each Other's Strengths to Work Around Each Other's Weaknesses

When you're working with a partner, whether it's in dance or in business, each person brings their own strengths and weaknesses to the table. According to Troels Bager, a World Professional Latin Dance Champion finalist, the best approach is to "turn your differences into strengths and learn from each other."[1] This is the way he works with his professional dance partner, Ina Jeliazkova. Recognize the weaknesses and then capitalize on the other's strengths. Find someone whose talent rewards areas that you are weak in.

Imagine two people teaming up, where one is really good on the financial side of the house and the other is good at marketing. The financial person, true to form, tends to be cautious, but sometimes misses out on taking full advantage of opportunities by under spending. The marketing person fits the stereotypical marketing mold – a risk-taker who finds opportunities, but who could wind up taking huge risks that add devastating costs.

---

1. Ina Jeliazkova and Troels Bager. Notes by author. Workshop and lessons / recordings. Virginia. September 18, 2016.

The secret to a good partnership for these two, and most real partnerships, is to create a balancing act. Recognize that you're different, but that you both want the same things, even though one of you is more cautious and the other is more of a risk-taker, or whatever your differences are.

There is more than one way of doing things in dance and in business. Take, for example, the accounting profession. There's not just one way of doing your chart of accounts or your taxes. If I were to put three CPAs in one room, I might get three different answers. The same is true in ballroom; different coaches offer different solutions to dance issues. Ina and Troels say that when they were World Amateur Champions transitioning to World Professional Finalists, there was a lot of pressure from the outside. They had to choose who to listen to and trust, and therefore, who not to. There is more than one approach, so listen to the feeling you get as people give you their advice. Trust it and take action.

Wherever you find conflict, success will usually require a mix of the approaches of both you and your partner. If you each recognize that your partner's position is valid and makes sense, you can build a compromise that winds up being the optimal blend of your strengths.

Even though my mother and I want the same things, we recognize that we have our differences. She estimates proposals for clients in her own unique way, as do I. We then have a collaborative session to compare approaches and arrive at a compromise. She focuses on the big picture, whereas I focus on the minor details; both are needed. If I am too immersed in the details, the chances of me overlooking other factors and considerations are high. By paying attention to each other, we employ the best aspects of both our approaches.

Combine Positive Qualities

In dancing you need to combine positive qualities in the same way that you do in business. This will lead to different kinds of routines, each featuring the strength of one of the partners and add a variety that will captivate judges and audiences.

In dance, couples are graded on how they hold each other. Observed factors include their symmetry, style, connection, and synchronicity. Do they move across the dance floor with confidence and power? Can they fully utilize their own space on a crowded floor without getting in the way of others?

Genya says that connection is extremely important both for beauty and safety. "When you are connected in dance and the man throws you, he **can** catch you – he knows where you are going to land," he says. "When you are disconnected, he can throw you but there is no guarantee you will be caught – he doesn't know how fast you will be going."

In companies, when people, processes and systems are connected, you know where they are heading and you have a better idea where they are going to land. When they are disconnected, you lack good visibility into the situation.

In business, if you are partnering with another company, start by evaluating your own company first. Make sure you are comfortable with where you are headed. Then with your partner, cross-check and make sure they are comfortable and have the same attitude and mindset; then you will be able to move forward. In particular, you must do this for both companies' cultures, because culture encompasses the behavior and attitude everyone will bring to the table, as well as a wide range of intangibles that can make a difference as to whether or not a partnership works.

Sometimes the business culture of one company doesn't match the business culture of another. That's okay; you don't have to work together. For example, my culture might have the intention of positively impacting society. Another business might have a culture of driving and generating revenue, no matter how many people they have to step on. As soon as you find there's a culture clash, let go of the idea of working together. A wide cultural divide will inevitably lead to failure, and you can either find a new partner or perform your strategy execution on your own.

Connection and Coordination

Whether you are dancing with a partner or working together in a business relationship, you want to make sure that not only are you connected, but that you and your partners are coordinated as well.

If you watch television dance competitions like *Dancing with the Stars* and *So You Think You Can Dance*, you probably already have some idea about what connection is. A lot of people think that connection in dance is just visual, through the eyes, or physical, making sure the bodies are connected through the arms and the frame. But, there is more to it than just these two items. There's an intellectual and spiritual connection that exists.

Observe how babies are able to connect. They detect and respond to visual and physical stimuli, yet they also respond to their caregivers' emotions and actions. Throughout the brain there are mirror neurons that help us tap into what other people are feeling. Humans are hardwired to connect.

In business, connection also comes from mindset. Let's say you are getting together with a partner. You should essentially "interview" each other to make sure your goals are going to be the same, that you are targeting the same vision and that you have the same attitude. If it becomes apparent that you are in step with each other, you're connected.

You also need to coordinate. In business, coordination is about unifying the activities, functions, and timings with the mission, goals, processes, and deadlines. For example, the sales and the delivery department need to coordinate so that goods and services take place according to the purchase order and statement of work.

In order to be coordinated, you need to be connected. In business, the functions and rhythms of departments may differ, but they still need to arrive at their destination together, with a shared mission, goals, and objectives. If the goal is to launch a new product within 6 months, marketing and production, among others, operate differently but need to end up at the same place at the same time. They must be connected, with the proper activities occurring in the right sequence. For example, marketing must start their campaign three months prior to launch in order to create a predictable pipeline of pre-orders so that production is better prepared come launch time. Marketing and production might not be truly in sync with how they do things, but they must be connected.

In business, effective connection and coordination require communication. You don't want to find yourself in a situation where one partner says to the other, "You never responded to this crisis," and the other answers, "I would have if you had let me know about it."

Commit to the Movement

As you're practicing and rehearsing and you're executing the strategy, you need to be able to commit to the movement, to be all in, whatever movement you're performing.

In dance, you are more committed when you are sure of the movement. If you're not confident, then you cannot commit. Yana mentions, "When practicing, you have to be aware of every moment that you are going through – physically and emotionally. Executing every technical point and being committed to the movement creates clarity and speed." [1]

Another facet is to move forward, but at the same time let go of control. You commit to what you're doing to the degree that you care about the result more than you care about how it happens. When your ego stays out of the way, natural things may happen that are very positive.

In business, this means giving everything and everyone room to breathe; in other words, trust them. Trust your process, your team, the people you're doing the beta test with, as well as whomever or whatever is involved with your strategy execution. When you don't trust, you wind up with a problem.

In my company, someone else oversees finance while I oversee marketing and relationships (clients and vendors). If I know my counterpart is not only good at finance, but that I trust our partnership, then I can let go of being in control and focus on my areas of expertise. That's not to say that if my gut instinct kicks in and tells me that something is not right on the finance part of an initiative, that I don't have a clarifying conversation with my colleague. But since I trust my partner, I can let go of being too controlling in an area that I'm not involved in.

Whether your partnership is with people within your organization or in different companies, you need to commit to and trust each other. If you can't do this, something is wrong and you need to fix it. Find out what the issue is and remedy it before it is too late. If you don't trust people, you end up micro-managing, butting heads, or communicating a message that you don't think the people you are working with are good enough. All of that leads to difficult relationships at best and messing up your strategy execution at worst.

---

1. Yana Mazhnikova. Interview by the author. Private lessons and recordings. Maryland. 2015-2016.

Or, maybe you don't trust the process itself. If this is the case, change the process or look at enough data so that your confidence increases. Don't wait until your testing is complete. Paying attention to a small sample size of data is sufficient to address your concerns.

Beth Kaplan is a competitive ballroom dancer who has also worked as General Manager or in the C-Suite at companies that include Rent the Runway, General Nutrition Centers, Bath & Body Works, and Procter & Gamble. She says that one of her dance teachers helped her learn to draw people in and get people to want to watch her performance. "It's that same thing at work," she says. "You have to have a certain emotional warmth and the soft skills of making people feel like they want to be part of what you're trying to achieve, because that's important." [2] When everyone's committed, without feeling controlled or controlling, that's exactly what happens.

Nonetheless, the team you are working with has to actually perform the tasks that they say they will do. Yana says that it's the same as with personal relationships. One thing a woman usually appreciates about a man is that he will put his hand on her shoulder and say, "Honey, don't worry, I will take care of it." This makes her feel safe, so she lets go of control and trusts. But he's got to do it; he has to be committed and he has got to deliver.

Persistence and Drive

One of the secrets to dance and business success is that you can't only rehearse and execute your strategy when it's fun. You have to make a consistent, long-term effort.

Persistence is key to attaining most worthwhile objectives. Realizing your goals and attaining success are the by-products of consistent persistence – working hard to accomplish what you want. Thomas Edison and Lincoln were persistent. Oprah was and is the same way.

The opposite of persistence is inconstancy or fickleness, where you apply yourself in a haphazard manner. This saps the energy out of your plan and will eventually lead to failure, or at the very least, an extremely long delay in getting what you want. If you quit and gave up, how would you feel later in your life not having achieved your goal?

2. Beth Kaplan. Interview by the author. Recording. Maryland. October 15, 2015.

Sometimes, people persist in a way that is draining and unproductive. If you find yourself feeling a lack of juice, stop pushing and decide to persist with patience and grace. You will free up bundled energy.

Persistence means continuous effort. It does not, however, guarantee continuous progress. Sometimes you persist and you run up against stumbling blocks. In dance there might be a step that takes too long; no matter how much you practice, you can't get to your next destination fast enough to go with the music. In business, you might discover you can't create a design that works within your budget.

These are times when you have to slow down and go back to the drawing board. Persistent people know that to progress forward sometimes you have to take two Cha Cha steps forward and one Cha step back.

If persistence is the key to your own personal success, possessing the motivation and drive to succeed is the key to persistence. Being driven is the result of maintaining your awareness of the love you have for what you are doing. If you love to dance and compete, then working out, going to practice and rehearsing will be enjoyable to you. The rituals for your dance workout, the small joys of taking each step, moving your hips and focusing on your posture, will become rewarding in themselves, as will the healthy glow that ignites within you. To become driven you need to identify all that you love and fill your life with that. Your excitement and enthusiasm will flow uncontrollably.

Find ways to accomplish your goals in ways that you enjoy. This will keep you motivated. For example, in my workout routines, I am not a big fan of aggressive muscle building exercises. However, I do like to increase my endurance slightly, while enjoying the outdoors, so I sometimes casually beach bike. I like to work on my flexibility – so I will do Barre and Pilates exercises. I like to work on my arms – but rather than lift weights, I choose to swim or kayak. By picking exercises that I enjoy, I can maintain my focus on building my strength to be a better dance performer – the art and sport that I love.

You need to do the same thing in business. In fact, your business model might evolve based on what you love to do. If you are given the task to transform an initiative or program, find what it is about that program that you love and focus your energy on putting more of that aspect into it. Focusing on what you love not only keeps you motivated; it also brings an additional layer of meaning to whatever you do.

In my business, I realized that I was motivated by helping governments and corporations plan and create strategies for their different initiatives. I was also driven by helping people understand the psychology behind decision making and the behavioral impacts those decisions have. I enjoyed finding ways to help people work within a partnership, as opposed to competing against each other. It gives me great satisfaction to help others achieve greater potential. It gives me meaning and fulfillment.

To remain motivated, I made sure my company prioritized what my team and I really care about – unity and helping clients achieve their mission.

To spice things up, we added several delivery methods to our portfolio. Instead of just working on projects or executive consulting, we also do speaking engagements, coaching and interactive workshop events.

Variety really is the best way to add fun. There are many ways to change up your routine. Make an effort to engage with others who are interested in your topic, simply by having fun dinner parties or joining (or creating) a meetup. Writing this book has been such a fun process for me. I've gotten to enjoy conversations with so many people on a topic that I am passionate about. It's a perpetually motivating journey for me to dance while dreaming up fun things to do to liven up my book and my business.

No matter what you're working on, everything has aspects that are tedious and repetitive. It's possible, however, to add variety to any monotonous activity. Celebrity trainer and nutritionist Shawn Rene Zimmerman, has me working out in different outdoor locations when the weather permits. Some days I train near the bay overlooking the calm water; other times I face the beach and watch the waves. I have a friend who works from home who makes work dates with different people at different cafes every week, especially when he's doing routine paperwork. Repetition with variation helps you maintain pleasure and contributes to your motivation. Look for opportunities to change where and how you do the more tedious aspects of what you need to do in order to accomplish your goal.

Even with a lot of variety, and after having cherry-picked the things you love most, there will be periods when you need to reignite your motivation. Life intervenes with fires to put out and stressful deadlines to meet, either in business or in your personal life; you can't help but get distracted. But the interruption doesn't have to last forever. For example, even though a string of major, multi-faceted projects – taking me to a new level in my business – distracted me from dancing for several years, I eventually found my way back because I still loved it. A few years ago, I found out that World Professional Latin Dance Champion, Yulia Zagoruychenko, was coming to Washington DC to perform. She is my idol; I had to be there to watch her performance. Because I was also there to join her workshop, I had the opportunity to meet with Riccardo Cocchi, her professional dance partner, and now seven-time World Professional Latin Dance Champion. Not only did Riccardo reignite my passion for dancing but he sparked the idea of writing about the parallel correlations between dance and business, which is how this book was born. The pleasure that I received from participating in the dance sport and being in that environment, even as a spectator, re-energized my motivation and enthusiasm and brought me back to dance. Sometimes we need to reignite our passion by being in the environment of what it is we love, even if it's just periodically going to workshops, lectures, lessons, or retreats.

Perfectionism

As I was working on this very chapter, I was planning a workshop retreat around the contents of this book. Part of promoting the event involved me doing a video shoot to get the message out on social media, contributing content to the website landing page, and much more. On top of that I was planning for a dance competition as well as working on a client document.

After receiving the edits from the videographer, I was horrified – the video didn't look like me at all. After I expressed my unhappiness, they wanted to charge me an extra few thousand dollars to retake it. I thought, "forget it." Even though I was faced with a time crunch, I said to myself, "How hard can it be?" So I buckled down and researched how to do my own shoot. I set myself up with a microphone plugged into my iPhone, which sat on a tripod, plus a remote video recorder. I used another tripod to hold an iPad with a teleprompter. I decided to use the lobby of my building as a backdrop but had to do it late at night so there would be no traffic. At 11 PM, I found myself (with the security guard as my lookout!) recording and re-recording my video almost 40 times while I tried to figure it all out. Finally – I did it. I nailed a take.

Was it perfect? No! But it was the best one out of them all. Of course, it was 2:30 AM already. My hair had become droopy, I was hot, twitchy, and my knee needed a rest after standing for so long. Nonetheless, I was extremely happy. I was proud that, not only did I learn something new; not only did I challenge myself to try my best – I simply got it done.

So yes I needed to take a Cha step back, face my obstacle, and work around deadlines and other commitments and then Cha Cha (push) forward. But, when you have a vision, there will always be obstacles. Those obstacles are what will test your true passion and purpose. That is when you discover if you are determined and driven enough to persistently overcome whatever stands in your way.

The key is not to look for perfection.

The content on my landing page wasn't perfect either. It needed grammar and other edits, but the marketing piece needed to move forward. So I had a decision to make – do I wait for my editorial support to give me the attention I need, which would result in a delay in social media campaign, or do I publish the retreat landing page and then work on the rest later? I did the latter. There is no perfection – there is just room for constant improvement. If I were to focus on perfection, I would not move forward in the manner that I wanted. Thankfully, I had learned to accept imperfection through dancing. There is no perfect performance – just a progression forward. It gets better and better each time.

Perfection can also de-motivate you in the rehearsal phase. Nobody's perfect. In the words of the late psychologist Carl Jung, "Perfection belongs to the gods; the most that we can hope for is excellence."

The search for perfection is an inflexible attitude, an attempt to force what can't be. It's a futile behavior that leads to procrastination and indecision.

Rather than aiming for perfection, strive for excellence instead. You can set high standards, and still achieve victory. Striving for excellence requires a strong internal reward system that focuses on the pursuit of satisfaction, pride, peace, joy, and fun. In the pursuit of excellence, you set realistic, flexible goals that act as road markers on your path. If you don't attain these standards, however, you can still win by yielding to your setbacks as lessons that will ultimately enable you to rise to greater heights.

Don't equate your self-worth with the outcome of the performance. Instead of constantly fearing failure, feel the joy of being in the arena and feel fortunate to have the talents and abilities you do have in order to compete, regardless of results. As for my challenge to learn how to produce videos, I felt fortunate to have access to technology and to learn something new. I didn't look at my video as a failure or setback but as a discovery.

Success is a roller coaster. It is impossible to be at a high point every day at every moment. You have to expect ups and downs. Improvement is a vital part of dance and business. Both are full of errors and setbacks. Joy comes from the process of learning from your mistakes, correcting them, and continually reaching and expanding your potential. My coaches help me embrace setbacks in performance as springboards for improvements in my dancing.

In business, executives that demand perfection create an environment filled with anxiety, tension, and fear. These obstacles stand in the way of productivity and performance. The environment that is created is not enjoyable. There is no job satisfaction. Perfectionist environments cause the surrounding talented people to sabotage themselves due to fear and criticism.

To overcome perfectionism, realize that you are still loved no matter what outcomes you achieve. It is acceptable to be less than perfect, even if this wasn't true in your childhood. What you feel is the result of how you view a situation; if you change your view, the feelings of tension and anxiety will change as well.

Transform your environment by creating a process where you give yourself and the people around you room to grow, learn, and produce. Beth says that real leadership isn't about having all the answers but rather the ability to solicit and to give back in a conversation. "If you think about a partnership on the ballroom floor," she says, "it's a lot about being able to give and receive information, and, as a result of that, being able to produce an outcome that is superior to one person trying to have all the content and all the answers and do all the leading all by themselves. I think that's something that just comes with practice and confidence."

She adds that the best results come when you're having a conversation about how to get from point A to point B, where you come in with an idea, then let the answer evolve. "It is not dissimilar to what happens as you're choreographing a routine, where one person in the partnership will have an idea, and you will work together on a particular figure or a sequence of music to get to something that is the best of each of your thought processes."

Change your attitude, make it fun to be around you, and people will gravitate towards you and want to match your enthusiasm as you strive for excellence and not perfection.

Constantly Challenge Yourself

In the dance world, you have to continue pushing your body or not only will you stagnate, you will lose ground. Your ability to make the movements you need to make requires constant practice.

Here's what Genya says:

"Because of the flexibility of moving, there are a lot of small muscle groups that need to be developed. They have to be engaged often. They have to be challenged all the time. That's why every single time you're going to end up doing more and more and more. It's never going to feel like you're done.

At the same time you're always going to be getting stronger and stronger and stronger.

The things I do today, I was not able to do a year ago and a year before that. From here, from now, I'll be able to do more. Even when I'm teaching dancing, I always try to do more. I constantly challenge my muscles. If I don't feel a slight pain, if the body doesn't feel a sense of being pulled and stretched, that's not a fulfilling day. When my body's slightly in pain, that's when I'm most happy. Like that feel good pain you get from working out at the gym or from hours of walking or jogging."

Just like in dance, if you want to have, not only a successful business, but one that helps you grow while having fun, you need to constantly stretch yourself. Continuously challenge your business muscles and they will get stronger and stronger.

If you turn weaknesses into strengths and use strenghts to differentiate yourself, you will be surprised at how far you can go.

Visualization

One of the tools that will allow you to enhance the value and the results of your rehearsal and strategy execution phase is visualization. When you practice it regularly, visualization will enable you to perform up to or beyond what you previously perceived as your potential. It works because it acts like a dress rehearsal. It is a form of mental practice that makes you familiar with the ideal script for the task ahead of you. When the time comes to execute what you have visualized, you have a sense that you have already experienced the moment or action you are taking and everything seems easier and already familiar.

Visualization also clears the mind of interfering, negative images that block your efforts to perform well by replacing them with images of success. You may be the best at what you do, but worries and negative images create anxiety and tension to hinder you. Positive images relax the mind and body so that you will perform well when you need to.

Visualization is an active form of meditation where you relax and choose to experience all your senses in your mind to influence your emotions and energy so you can respond positively to events in your life. What you see, hear, feel, smell, or taste in your mind's "eye" can strongly influence your beliefs and achievements.

One of the reasons visualization works is because the brain cannot distinguish between real and imagined information and experiences; it sees and accepts all images and events as if they were real. For example, imagining a delicious meal can literally make your mouth water.

In dance (or any other sport), the losses and the victories are the result of the visions and images that the players, often unconsciously, carry with them. If you have an image of yourself blowing a lead, missing a turn, or forgetting a pattern, you will create tension and anxiety that will contribute negatively to your performance. On the other hand, if you carry around mental images of success, you create an inner state of calm, confidence, and relaxation that contributes positively to actual success.

Legendary professional golfer Jack Nicklaus, in his book, *Golf My Way*, talks about having very sharp, distinct images in his mind prior to each shot. "First I 'see' the ball where I want it to finish, nice and white and sitting up high on bright green grass. Then the scene quickly changes and I 'see' the ball going there: its path, trajectory, and shape, even its behavior on landing. Then there is a sort of fade-out, and the next scene shows me making the kind of swing that will turn the previous images into reality." [1]

Shawn Rene teaches that visualization and physiology is key to getting back into focus when you have trouble with a certain routine. "Visualize yourself mentally and physically performing the routine perfectly," she says. "You have to mentally focus and visualize it first to produce it physically." [2]

A significant factor in visualization is to imagine the emotional experience that comes with the success you expect to achieve. Shawn Rene says this is important because the hypothalamus, the emotional center of the brain that receives neuropeptides (the chemical messengers of hormones), transforms emotions into physical responses. Emotions, combined with visualization, helps connect the creative with the intuitive part of the brain that we use less frequently than the logical part. "By yielding to the creative side we actually restore balance in the brain," she says. "This allows access to the mind-body connection to achieve your desired goal. This part of the brain automatically steers you to your goal."

It is about connecting to your feelings. When I dance, it is important to connect to the emotion of the dance. Most try to focus only on the technique and skill, but it is important to develop the emotions as well.

Before you start to visualize, it's good to get yourself into a very relaxed state. Many people do this by combining breathing exercises with progressive relaxation. (For instructions on how to do these, see Chapter 2.)

---

1. Jack Nicklaus. *Golf My Way* (New York: Simon & Schuster, 2005), 79.
2. Shawn Rene Zimmerman. Interview by author. Notes / documentation. Delaware, August 2015.

Once you feel relaxed enough, visualize in great detail what it is you want to experience, from the beginning to victory celebration. Shawn Rene offers these suggestions to her clients:

- When performing visualization exercises, it is important to focus on how you look and feel when you perform your best. Visualization is a form of mental rehearsal. When you actually execute the movements, the body will act as though it has already performed them.

- The more specific the intention, the more specific the results. Whatever you believe is what your body will do. So when you think of your intention make sure it is positive, specific, detailed, and clear.

- Imagine *everything* related to your successful accomplishment, including the praise and the results afterwards. For example, if you're a swimmer, you might imagine yourself winning and receiving a gold medal, with the crowd screaming your name as you receive it. In business, if you work for someone else, you might see your bonus check and your boss showing you the view from your new office that comes with your promotion.

- The key is to visualize that you already have the goal accomplished that you want. This is a mental trick. You don't hope you'll achieve it, or build confidence that someday it will happen. You "live and feel it" as if it is happening to you now. Your subconscious will act upon the images you create within, regardless of whether those images reflect your current reality or they are a goal that you are aiming for.

Research shows that we change brain structure through repetition of visualization. According to Dr. David R. Hamilton, brain scans showed the same degree of changes in the same areas of the brain whether people were actually playing the piano or were just imagining playing the piano in their mind.[1] Those changes required repetition of the finger movements, even if they were only imaginary. In both cases, these regions in the brain will shrink when the work is stopped. Thus, continuous visualization practice is necessary to obtain the best results.

---

1. David R. Hamilton PhD, *Does your brain distinguish real from imaginary?*, http://drdavidhamilton.com/does-your-brain-distinguish-real-from-imaginary/, Published October 30, 2014.]

Now, let's apply these practices to our "Business Minds." Before you visualize, accept that something needs *transformation* (Chapter 1). Then use *insight* to recognize where you currently are (Chapter 2). Next create a *strategy map* as to what you will visualize (Chapter 3). Finally, *execute your strategy* and create an ongoing visualization practice (Chapter 4).

Affirmations

Affirmations are a very useful corollary to visualization. They are conscious, preplanned, positive thoughts to direct your actions and behaviors in a productive way. Unless you direct and control your own thoughts you leave much to chance.

With affirmations, you can change patterns of negative thought that, like tape recordings in your head, continue to play old, counterproductive tunes. Affirmations help you develop your full potential with new, positive phrases. Typically they start with the words, "I am" followed by a positive quality such as "focused" or something specific you envision, like "an online millionaire."

Words truly can transform the quality of your existence. Dr. Andrew Newberg and neuroscience researcher, Mark Robert Waldman, write in their book, *Words Can Change Your Brain*, "The ways we choose to use our words can improve the neural functioning of the brain." But, you also need to support the affirmation with realistic thoughts. "Positive words and thoughts propel the motivational centers of the brain into action," they add. "By thinking in this way, you stimulate frontal lobe activity. This area includes specific language centers that connect directly to the motor cortex responsible for moving you into action." [1] You can't just say the words "independently wealthy" while you are also sarcastically thinking, "Oh yeah right, like that is going to happen." You need to feel that what you are affirming is possible so that it can find a way to occur. Once you have triggered the possibilities in your mind, you will attract opportunities because you are more alert, ready to receive them, and willing to take action.

---

1. Newberg, Andrew and Waldman, Mark Robert. *Words Can Change Your Brain.* 12 Conversation Strategies to Build Trust, Resolve Conflict, and Increase Intimacy. New York: Hudson, 2012.

Affirmations are most effective if, as you recite each one, you take thirty seconds to visualize what the affirmation is saying. If you affirm, "I am a national champion," see yourself winning an important event. Feel what it would be like to be such a star.

Affirmations turn doubt into confidence, increase your concentration, prevent you from pushing yourself too hard or becoming frustrated, reduce self-criticism, sharpen your skills, help you cope with fatigue, treat injuries, and carry out any other performance tasks that you may need to address. During times when you are particularly self-critical, if you consciously choose loving, caring phrases, you can help yourself change the negativity you feel. Tell yourself "I am talented, intelligent, and creative," or "I deserve the best," or "I am abundant and have a lot to offer." Or you can use a mantra, typically one word that embodies whatever you are striving for. Mantras are something you can repeat throughout the day without any setup as a needed reminder. You might say "tall, tall, tall" if you're working on your posture or elongation, or "love, love, love" if you're trying to be more accepting of yourself or to display compassion to others.

It's worthwhile to utilize visualization, affirmations, or mantras concurrently. "The more parts of your brain and senses you use, the more impactful it will be," says Shawn Rene. "Visualization is using all of your senses: seeing, hearing, smelling, tasting, and touching. You speak affirmations out into existence. Combining mental and verbal communication increases the creativity in the brain."

Anchoring

When you reach the point of your visualization where positive feelings are at their peak, bookmark that feeling so you can easily go back to it. This is accomplished by associating your state of mind with a word, an image, or most commonly, a physical gesture or position – any of which is called an anchor. After you implement your anchor, you are able to summon these feelings any time you want. This technique is used in neuro linguistic programming, a personal development system based on a combination of psychotherapy and hypnosis, originally developed by Richard Bandler and John Grinder.

Create an anchor when, for example, you're seeing and hearing the crowd roar its approval while you receive your medal or when you feel a tremendous sense of peace and love. Whatever you're working with, make an effort to heighten the feelings by filling your body with them from the top of your head all the way down to your toes. Then imagine yourself in three different scenes from your life where you feel the way that you do from this visualization, one that involves seeing, one that involves hearing, and one that involves touch. For example, you could see the ballroom, then imagine dancing while you're hearing the music, and then finally while physically holding your reward trophy in your hands. Correlate seeing all the objects there, and feeling this way. Imagine standing and taking a victory photo with your trophy in your hand. Tune in and notice what part of your body holds the largest quantity of this feeling and place your hand there. Say to yourself, "From now on, any time I place my hand on this very spot of my body, I feel this way." If you prefer, instead of touching a part of your body, you can use a word or an image.

If this sounds unusual, the truth is we use anchors, which are really mental patterns of association, all the time in life. One of my grandmother's best friends ended up having an impact on my dancing. As a child I heard her share this story and it stuck with me – whenever she wanted to win an argument with her husband, she would go and put on red lipstick to ready herself for "battle." I noticed that in the last two weeks before the performance of one particular show dance, I was looking for red lipstick to match my outfit. I found the perfect one. I would come into practice, and I would put on that red lipstick. Even when I wasn't wearing my costume dress, or anything, I was dancing so much better when I put on that lipstick.

I've coached businesses who transitioned to a cloud model, allowing their employees to work virtually for the first time. For some, the new, office-free situation was difficult to adjust to. One employee actually needed to put on a suit to be able to work and function. Before closing a deal, he would put on his favorite power tie to wear alone in his basement. Nonetheless, because this tie was an anchor for him, he would get favorable results!

There is a great deal of power in consciously using anchors to help you reach your goals. Remember to use your anchor on a daily basis for a week, to create a habit and ensure the benefits of your visualizations stick with you. You can use anchors to help you feel most secure and confident, or loving and peaceful, before rehearsals, meetings, performances, or any stressful situation.

Dressing Up

The rehearsal period is also when you figure out your costumes. Costumes are an important part of every performance. You have to test what you're wearing because it might not be as easy to move in or as comfortable as you need. The wrong costume can also affect you emotionally. "There was one costume, it was a beautiful costume," says Yana, "but it didn't fit my personality. My emotional state in this costume was absolutely terrible. I felt very uncomfortable. I went to a vendor and I changed the costume, and when I changed it I danced so much better. You could see the difference, and it was amazing."

How a costume looks is obviously important. It's your branding and your image. Yana and her former partner received a review in *Dance Beat* magazine after a fourth or fifth place finish that showed how important this is. "It said something like 'This couple should be much higher in my opinion, but the girl needed to update her costume.'"

Yana says that even though on some level the reviewer should have just focused on her dancing, she understands how the reviewer could have made that point. "I think why they were saying that was that the element of surprise, and being new and interesting, was gone because they've seen me in that costume already a few times."

In business, your costume is your website, your copywriting, your packaging, your pitch, and anything else related to the look and feel of your marketing. It's the wrapping paper that customers have to unwrap in order to connect with your product or services. My brother, who studied at both Temple University's Tyler School of Art, Japan campus and the Rhode Island School of Design (RISD), advised me to slow down while I was opening my first iPhone package. He pointed out the thoughtfulness that went into the tremendous detail of the packaging, which is a hallmark of all Apple products. Many other companies focus on various areas of their presentation. Car manufacturers spend significant time on making the experience of shutting a car door more appealing. One of the things that attracted me to my BMW is the calmness of how the door shuts.

This is the kind of design culture you want to have. Design is worth your attention as it can influence sales. Websites, for example, get outdated every few years as design styles change. An out of date website can send a message to customers that your company is not up with the times and doesn't care about the details.

Split test everything you are using to market your transformation. Use small samples of two different approaches to see which version gets a higher response. It's easy to send traffic to a website using Google Adwords. One famous author spent $200 to test several different book titles, which are a kind of a costume for a book, this way. There were six in his Adwords test, including *Millionaire Chameleon* and *Broadband and White Sand*. You've never heard of either of those books. On the other hand, you probably are aware of a huge bestseller called *The 4-Hour Workweek*. The $200 that Tim Ferriss used to test book names clearly paid off.

I also asked my friends to test the website landing page for my workshop retreat. I wanted to know if my messaging emotionally connected. By using a small data sample, I was able to receive valuable feedback.

Take a Step Back to See What You Can Improve

As you're progressing forward, it's important, even when you're close to your performance or your launch, to take a step back and notice if there's anything that needs improving. Sometimes there's a nagging doubt that you just don't want to admit is there; be courageous enough to deal with it.

On the other hand, sometimes nagging doubts are just meaningless claptrap from your inner critic.

How can you figure out which is which?

Here's a fun kinesthetic exercise, called a "dance walk," to help. The physical objective is to transfer your weight from your back leg to your front leg.

Get up now and do this. Simply put one leg in front of the other, and put your weight on your back leg. Then slowly change where you hold the weight from the back leg to the front one.

You'll notice, as you transfer the weight, that there's a point where the weight isn't on either leg, but in the middle.

Now do the exercise again. Imagine your back leg is the past, your middle is the present, and your front leg is the future. Pretend the weight on your back leg is your nagging doubt. As you transfer your weight from your back legs to your hips, pretend you are "pulling" information from the past to the present. When you are ready to transfer your weight to your front leg, drop your hips as if you are dropping excess pieces of information that you don't need or, dropping unnecessary doubt. As you land, you connect to the future, only keeping the information you need.

Sometimes, when something feels wrong, you may not be able to come up with the solution on your own. In the dance world, coaches are indispensable. Many times you can't see what you're doing wrong on your own. I needed a coach to help me figure out what was wrong during the "alemana" turn within my Rumba dance. I needed to be told that I was turning my head and body all at the same time instead of breaking down my turn. Now that I understand what not to do, I am consciously aware of it and why I had been doing it, so I can focus on what I need to do.

Today we are inundated with information from a wider range of sources than ever before, which can lead to difficult decisions about which to keep and use, and which to throw away. This is not an easy question to answer on a regular basis; that is why we suffer from information overload.

However, once you understand how to break things down, becoming aware of what information is necessary to retain and to drop what you cannot control, it becomes easier. Here are two items that are worth focusing on:

1. **Pay attention to your partner's steps -** In partnership dancing, we tend to focus so much on our own steps, that we don't pay attention to our partner's steps. We need to become aware of where our partner is and where they are going. A partner could be anyone you are working with to obtain and share information. Partners can be your employees,

vendors, leadership, clients, distributors, resellers, external sources, etc. So if you are in marketing, become aware of where production is in their process and where they are going. If you are launching a new product, become aware of where your competition is and where they seem to be going.

2. **Make sure your story is the star of your show, not your technique -** When we present ourselves in dancing and in business, we are sharing a story based on our vision. But when we get stuck in technical details, we forget what we are trying to represent. So when external sources are watching and evaluating (judges, shareholders, media, etc.), we don't want them to be looking at technique, but instead the overall picture, the message. Techniques are just the tools to relay the story, the picture, and the message. For example, I am currently working on an Argentine Tango showcase dance. The Tango flicks, in the dance, are the lower leg movements based on the lady's footwork in the Argentine Tango; this is technique. But the message and story of my dance is important – who is seducing who? Am I seducing the man or vice versa? And what happens at the end; do they leave together or does she leave him?

Accept the Scenic Route

You won't always be able to just follow a straight road to success. There is always some street that is closed for repairs. That's okay. Notice that virtually anything good that has come your way in business or in life has usually taken longer for you to arrive at than you would have liked. When you try to accelerate the process, you experience setbacks. Don't try hard to get results. They come in time with good, consistent, patient efforts.

Uber's driverless cars will not succeed, step by step, in a straight line. They're already hitting some unexpected curves and side roads. Before they reach certain milestones, let alone their ultimate goal of a driverless taxi-type system, they'll have to pause and readjust to get back on track.

Sometimes the step back (or sideways or forward) is an external situation. The market changes. Genya and I were supposed to go to France to perform and compete outside of Paris. Unfortunately, a terrorist attack happened on November 13th, 2015, the night of my birthday. Even though we were supposed to be there at the end of November, it just didn't feel comfortable for us to go there and perform. This was something that was caused by the outside world, which in other cases might be called, the market. So even though we had a goal of performing internationally, and at the time, I hadn't done a competition with Genya, we canceled our plans. It was a major setback.

Rather than letting our decision to stay in the U.S. deter us, we took a step back in order to make a plan that would move us forward. We decided to do a local showcase where we would perform a Paso Doble. We had five weeks to mentally and physically prepare, come up with the choreography, to rehearse, and finally, to perform.

Losing the opportunity to dance at the Paris competition wasn't part of our plan. It was out of our control, but it ultimately led to growth. Our alternative came about because we were committed to our intention of doing something artistically together. We had to come back full circle to that intention as we reevaluated our plans. Remembering your intention is important. It will help you continue in the right direction, and no matter what setbacks you may have, you will be okay.

Even your new plans can run into difficulties. Be flexible, make changes, but understand the impact and the risk. I certainly had to adapt during the rehearsal for our performance. During one rehearsal, I twisted my ankle. The very next day my knee gave out. Years before this, I had had ACL surgery, so I had to be VERY careful moving forward.

Once again, we reevaluated, cautiously. I had to add some knee exercises and change the way that I was rehearsing due to where I was with my body. I also had to make sure I was comfortable with the routine; anything that might be injurious to my knee needed to be changed.

Things happen. But we were still committed.

Ultimately, in spite of the tight schedule and all the changes we had to make, our performance went off without a hitch. The audience responded enthusiastically, and my personal growth as a dancer skyrocketed. I grew as a person as well. Each time you overcome adversity, you become stronger, more flexible and patient, and more accepting of whatever comes your way – which makes it easier to handle everyday life in a more graceful way, no matter what shows up.

You can be sure that opportunity is going to show up. In dance, it's a performance. In business, it's a launch, campaign, or some kind of presentation. In any case, it's what we've been leading up to. In Chapter 5, we'll talk about the ins and outs of seizing the opportunities you've been dancing towards.

Don't look at your feet to see if you are doing it right.
Just Dance.

– ANNE LAMOTT

You earn your trophies at practice.
You just pick them up at competitions.

– UNKNOWN

CHAPTER 5

PERFORMING AT COMPETITION

Launch

Congratulations. This is it. After all your hard work, it's time to make your move. In business, this is the moment when you launch the transformational change you've been working on. In dance, it's competition time.

For ballroom dancers, the day of the competition starts with how you prepare the night before. You may watch some inspiring dance videos and run through the choreography in your mind before you go to bed. Create a feeling of anticipation for yourself, with the knowledge that tomorrow is your big day.

In addition to physical preparation, such as getting proper sleep, there is also a mental preparation of "owning it" as if you are the star of the competition, performing at the level of a champion, full of confidence and pride. This optimistic attitude shows in your gestures, postures, and intentions. Without the proper intentions, you might seem arrogant and snooty. Tune into what you want to "give" and "gain" at each performance.

My attitude towards a dance competition or performance is that "I am going to give my best performance, I worked hard for this, and I am going to do the best for me, and I am going to have a lot of fun while inspiring others." Yana suggests that, "The mindset needs to be 'This is for you and for you only, you deserve to enjoy it.' The audience doesn't care how hard you worked, how you got there, and how much you paid for the costume; they are there to see your performance. Be prepared if judges make comments, take it as constructive criticism. It is not easy being a judge – respect them."

On competition day, there are a variety of steps to getting ready. You need to stretch and do your warm-ups. There's putting on your makeup (or shaving if you're a man), styling your hair and getting dressed. While you're performing these activities, use the time to get into the proper mood. When Yana competes she gets into the mood by singing. Find what works for you.

Dasha Sushko, a former 5-time Russian National Dance Champion who is currently a national and world competition judge, says this about the day of the performance: "I need certain time to prepare myself mentally, to do makeup, hair, and dress. I need certain music to be playing. Before even walking on to the dance floor, I feel good. As a dancer and performer, I would suggest you know what makes you feel good and try this even before you go on the dance floor. It will help you a lot if you feel good while you're preparing."[1]

Genya takes a different approach. He says that on performance day, you have to save your emotional energy. "You're concentrating from the moment you wake up," he says. "Sometimes you get into this trance, where you almost catch yourself sometimes not eating. You go by your competitive friends, and you don't even say hello. Not because you don't want to say hello, because you're so focused. You have to build the right amount of enthusiastic energy about going on the floor. Not burned out."

In business, you also want to be aware of what makes you feel good, with proper nutrition, exercise, and sleep. Be especially vigilant on the night before your performance.

Eating and sleeping the right amounts are important for everyone at all times, but it is especially important when you are trying to accomplish something. Arianna Huffington writes about the importance of a good night sleep to elevating your business performance in both her books, *Thrive* and *Sleep Revolution*. She says a lack of sleep negatively affects productivity, energy level, and decision making. There are losses in the areas of creativity, memory consolidation, the ability to learn and solve problems, the capacity to deal with stress and anxiety, and the functioning of the immune system. Loss of sleep increases your risk of a heart attack, a stroke, diabetes, and obesity.

You probably won't warm up for business the way dancers do. Instead, try a visualization of what it is you will be performing, with everything working the way you desire. It's also worth grooming yourself with a little extra care, which shows your mind that you mean business today. Finally, put

---

1. Dasha Sushko. Interview by author. Recording Delaware and New Jersey. February 2016.

yourself in the best mood or headspace for accomplishment while you are getting ready and even on your drive to work. You could play music, work out, meditate; do whatever helps you feel calm, comfortable, and in control.

Getting the Details Right on Performance Day

Nothing can hamper your mood on the day of a performance or launch like being unprepared. In dance, if you're a woman, make sure you've gone to your hair colorist and stylist just the right number of days before your performance so your hair will look its best. Same with your nails and tanning. Test your outfit to make sure you move well in it. Leave enough time for alterations so that you don't have to pick it up the day of the performance. Look through your makeup to make sure you have everything you could possibly need without making a last minute stop at the nearest Sephora.

There are some things you have to take care of the day of the performance, like ordering your video from the hosting organization, so you can review it afterwards. But the rest of your tasks should be pre-set.

In business, your launch may involve a product, presentation to a group or an individual, a tradeshow or a speaking engagement, so some of the advance preparation is the same. You want your appearance to be worry free and taken care of ahead of time. Also, make sure you're ready with your giveaways for the trade show, or leave behinds after your presentation. Most of all, be prepared for how you will follow up post event. If you are there to capture leads, have a lead capture process in place so that you can properly execute it the day of the event.

If you are doing a launch that doesn't involve a presentation, you need to prepare ahead of time as well. A communication plan must be in place that is synchronized with everyone involved, for instance the legal department, the marketing department, production or human resources. If you are launching a new product, production must be stocked with parts, the delivery department must be ready, and marketing must be conveying what will happen so production and delivery can be properly timed. If you're consulting for a client or partner, you want to make sure a well-thought-out transition plan is generated as part of the launch to avoid disruption.

In business, as in dance, the more prepared you are for your performance, the more relaxed and confident you will be when you perform.

Beware of Expectations

When you visualize yourself performing like a champion or as the star of the competition or your business performance, be careful not to set up expectations for a specific result, such as a first place dance showing, sales of a certain amount, or closing the deal. You may be banking on these things, as if they were guaranteed to happen. But these kinds of expectations block your development and limit your horizons. They distract you from the task at hand because you are too busy looking forward to your dream of the future. Thinking ahead to very specific results, which are out of your control, can lead you to becoming unfocused, un-centered, pressured and anxious; this will interfere with your performance.

If it happens that you don't meet your expectations for specific outer results, you could be in for a severe disappointment that can slow your future progress as you lick your emotional wounds. This has happened to me in the past, where I was sure I would win a proposal submission. My company had the location for the contract work rented out, we had on-boarded the team, and done the due diligence work for preparing; we were ready to go. The client had stressed the sense of urgency and we were fully prepared, until we received the devastating news that we did not win the contract. The impact was severe. We had not prepared a fallback position for if we didn't win. We spent months letting people go, attempting to break our lease for the unused space without a penalty, and seeking other opportunities.

On the other hand, when you free yourself from preconceived notions, you open yourself up to endless possibilities and opportunities. You are free to change and create enormous personal and business power because you allow yourself to see and understand yourself and your world as it really is. When you put aside expectations, you accept that you can't control your future, only influence it. This kind of thinking increases the odds that you will give one of your better performances.

Change Your Expectations to Preferences

There's nothing wrong, however, with aiming for and having a preference to succeed at a particular goal. Preferences lead to better results than expectations. A preference presupposes that you have less concern for the outcome, yet you direct your efforts along the path of excellent performance. You keep yourself open to possibilities for greater expansion rather than limit yourself with defined expectations.

If you prefer a positive outcome as opposed to expect, and then the event does not happen as predicted, you will be less disappointed. As I was preparing to host a workshop retreat on executive transformation there was a snowstorm that delayed my plans; I had to be flexible enough to make some alterations.

This turned out, however, to be fortuitous. The new venue turned out to be a better location, centrally located near both an airport and a train station, and close to Baltimore and Washington, D.C. Plus, the facility was more suited to conferences and meetings.

See your preferences as guides whose job it is to keep you on the path of excellence and success.

In business, particularly in the corporate world, there is a huge emphasis based on management by expectation. When we evaluate performance, we use measures, metrics, and key performance indicators (KPIs) as a means of motivating sales, marketing, and management to produce. These measurements often represent unrealistic expectations that, just like in dance, create unnecessary anxiety and pressure, factors that limit and block performance. Companies like Accenture, Microsoft, Adobe, Google, Expedia, and Motorola have recently re-evaluated their HR performance measurements for this very reason. The changes made are focusing more on having more effective communication, better management strategy plans, and stronger execution.

Winning

Just like expectation, a focus on winning or accomplishment is an end game. It can take the lifeblood out of the experience you are going through. You can have an experience of greater value by viewing what you are doing as a journey. Go through the process focused on quality. Are you living your journey with fun and enjoyment? Even in business you can enjoy the process of seeing something come to life. It could be a marketing initiative, new software, or even doing something with greater efficiency. By letting go of winning as the objective, you focus on the moment and the inner gratification of accomplishing what you are performing as you do it.

"We do want good results," says Dasha, "but I always say, don't concentrate on results. Concentrate on good dancing. The results will come. Usually it works because if you concentrate on 'I want the results, I want to be in the final,' it's not a good goal."

But if winning is not important, then why keep score? Keeping score gives insight into your performance level throughout the event and gives an indication of how you are progressing over a period of time. And it is fun to win. But being *free* of the *need* to win results in greater personal power and performance. Let the possibility of winning keep you alert and sharp. If you win, terrific; if not, feel the joy and satisfaction of having participated. Focus on how well you are mastering specific skills. Notice how the event provides you with an opportunity to display your skills against challenging competition.

You can use winning as a way to focus on your skills while you are practicing. Develop your ability so that you have the potential to win. You can't control the results for any particular competition, but you can make yourself good enough to know you are in the running. Dasha tells her students they need to push themselves if they want to succeed. "Work harder and harder, and harder," she says. "If you train hard, if you spend enough time in the studio concentrating on what you need to do and practicing what the teachers taught you, then the results and the winning will come, but if you don't do what you need to do, it's not going to be there."

Over the course of his career, Genya's goals have changed. Three years ago he was hungry to win. Sometimes he was successful, sometimes he lost, but eventually he discovered something. "It often happens that you will win the competition but you really didn't like the way you danced," he says. "And then you dance the best you ever danced in your life, and you lose the competition."

That experience changed his approach. "To me, it's important to achieve my personal goal in dance. It doesn't mean a placement. It's this thing that you're working on specifically at this period of time. Let's say you're working on technique or you're working on presentation or you're working on musicality. If you can go on the next competition and achieve that certain part of your dancing, you bring it to a different level. That, to me, is winning."

Genya says he is less attached to making it to a world final than when he was younger. "At this point I just want to enjoy it because I know I don't have ten years ahead of me anymore," he says. "I have maybe one or two left as a professional competitive dancer. So, I'm just enjoying it at this point and that's all I want to do."

Win or lose, you have to dig deep and discover other aspects of your essence. Prizes and victories are fleeting, while outstanding performances, regardless of the outcome, are tremendously rewarding. "There are no standards and no possible victories except the joy you are living while dancing your run," writes Fred Rohe, in *The Zen of Running*. "In any life, joy is only known in the moment – now! So feel the flow of your dance and know you are not running for some future reward – The real reward is now!"

After my own competition in May of 2015, I spoke to Allan Tornsberg, world renowned choreographer and coach of Cheryl Burke, who performed as a professional on *Dancing with the Stars*. Allan had judged my performance that afternoon, so I asked how he thought I performed and if he had any feedback for me. His answer was, "You looked like you were having fun, were you?" And yes, I was!

The fun in competition on the day of the performance is not about the winning, but the preparation to get on the dance floor, then performing and moving or inspiring the audience and judges and letting them cheer you on. There is also fun in the preparation. Finally, there's the fun of walking on the dance floor as though you ARE the winner, which you already are! Regardless of the outcome, focus on the satisfaction of having performed so well.

One time a dance teacher told me that he came in sixth place dancing with one of his top-level students. You'd think he would find that disappointing, but it was one of the most positive memories of his dance life. He said that sixth place for him was such a good place because the audience loved the dance. They applauded every time he and his partner would come close to a corner. They received many compliments from judges. The skill level was not as high as the people he competed against, but he felt really, really good dancing. That's the feeling you need to go for at a competition. If you feel good about dancing, and people like it, that's the number one thing.

For everybody, the goal is different. Sometimes you just need to compare yourself with yourself. At one point I had had knee surgery, and just the fact that I could be on the dance floor and not fall, was a winning accomplishment for me. In business, something others might find small might be a milestone accomplishment depending on how you as an individual, business, or company have succeeded based on where you were months ago.

Detachment

Letting go of your attachment to winning and achievement may be perfectly fine in theory, but it's not easy to do. Detachment doesn't mean that you cease to care about a dance or business event. The outcome is a gauge that measures, at least to a certain extent, your level of improvement, although sometimes you can watch a video and you will think you did better than the judges thought you did – or vice versa. In either case, accept your performance for what it truly is.

Detachment also means letting go of all the ego ramifications that we attribute to success. A loss – or a victory, for that matter – is never a measure of your self-worth as a dancer or decision maker. By practicing detachment, your perspective on your dance sport or your business is healthier. You can love it with passion, yet see it as only a microcosmic event in a universe of activities.

When I talk with decision makers who are struggling with transforming their business, I ask them to recall how often they have fun at work. Most respond by saying, "Fun?" as they look at me with puzzled eyes. But for most, fun is what attracted them to their line of work – a fun challenge.

Over time, however, they lost the ability to detach themselves from the business game and its outcome. Their emotional involvement reduced the level of joy they were able to experience in business activities. They lost the awareness of the beauty of the game. This loss can often have a negative impact on results. In business, when you are attached only to outcomes, your performance declines, just like in dance. Your productivity decays and you lose your enthusiasm for the joy of delivery.

To detach, ask yourself, "What do I love about my _____?" Fill in the blank – your business, or dance, or whatever it is that you want to detach from the need for results. Then, focus on your passion. Stay in the present moment and be with what is happening now. Just enjoy the journey.

For certain people, starting the process of detachment can take some extra effort. If you're having trouble detaching from your expectations of winning, here's an exercise you can do.

1. Start by taking a few deep breaths, in and out.

2. Return to your natural breath and mentally bring yourself to a place in nature where you feel at peace. It doesn't matter whether this is a place you've been to in the past or an imaginary place. Notice what you see, hear, feel, and smell in this place.

3. When you are as relaxed as possible, ask your imagination or your unconscious to come up with a symbol for what you are attached to. If nothing comes, you can create one on your own. For a dance competition, this might be a trophy. For a sales goal, it might be a big green dollar sign. For a promotion, it might be a throne or a crown.

4. Now imagine a winged creature coming towards you. It could be a bird that is real, like an eagle or a hummingbird, or it could be something from the world of imagination, like a Pegasus or a flying dragon.

5. Imagine that this winged being has a gift for you in its mouth or beak. It could be a parchment with some words on it or an object like a pen, a ball of light or just some color. The creature releases what it has for you and you take it. You may know exactly what their gift means, or you may have to wait for later to be inspired with the answer at exactly when you need it. And if no gift shows up, don't worry – you don't need one at this time.

6. In return, or just because you want to, you give your symbol to the winged creature.

7. He or she flies it up to the sun with your symbol.

8. The symbol burns away in the sun.

9. As it burns in the sun, it transforms into purple droplets, or any color you want, which sprinkle over you like rain.

10. One of these droplets enters you heart. Feel it fill your heart with peace or love or whatever positive quality you need. Notice that you are filled with as much of this quality as you have ever needed. Because of this, you experience an unconditional happiness or joy or a simple peace. When you have this feeling, winning or losing, achievement or failure is meaningless. You already have all the happiness and peace you will ever need.

11. Put your hand on your heart and know that any time you need help feeling this way, you can place your hand at the center of your chest and you will feel this way again.

12. Enjoy this state for as long as you'd like, then take a few breaths and open your eyes and return to everyday awareness.

For Today, Let Go of Perfectionism and Just Be Aware

Perfectionism has its place. While you're rehearsing, it helps to notice every detail so that you can do as many things as well as possible. Just don't be so much of a perfectionist that you forget to notice all the great things you are already doing.

On the day of your performance, as you are getting ready to go before the judges or launch your business transformation, perfectionism is just another item to detach from.

Last minute changes are usually about trying to be overly perfect. It's important to ask whether what you're evaluating is really necessary **this** minute. Can it be taken care of down the road, in other iterations or refinements of what you're doing? If it's not a performance threatening imperfection or mistake, such as a typo in your ad that lists the wrong price or location, just note the lesson learned in your awareness and write it down so you can make it part of your post-performance review, which will be covered in Chapter 6. Hold on to that list so that next time around you will do better and better. Nothing's ever perfect.

If I'm conducting a business retreat, it will never be an impeccably perfect retreat. No matter how good it is, it can get better each time I do it.

If you have a marketing launch announcement, or a Super Bowl ad, or an efficiency improvement, it will never be as perfect as you would like because things around you are also changing. If I use a particular neuroscience example in my retreat, my example could suddenly become outdated by a news story of a scientist's discovery that comes out the morning of the retreat while I'm too busy to pay attention to the media. This is outside of my control.

Everything constantly gets better. There's always room for improvement; the needs of the market are ever evolving. As this book is being written, Windows is on version 10 and iPhone 7 just launched and some celebrity is on her 47th new look with a different hairstyle and color and wardrobe. And do you know what? That's all great. It would be boring if conditions always remained the same and no one was forced to change.

There is no perfect dance. Your performance is ever evolving, but you just want it to become better and better than what you were. Monitor your stress level in competition and beyond. If you're going to change a last minute step (or even worse, something that is a large part of the routine), you will exhaust yourself, stress yourself out, and maybe even forget what the new change is. Your partner might do the new change while your muscle memory kicks in and you inadvertently perform the old choreography. That would be an unfortunate mistake that could easily be averted by not making the change at all.

This is true in business as well. Last minute changes increase your risk of making a bigger mistake. They also cost more. Rework exhausts resources. Remember that the next time you think of making a last-second change in your business.

The Courage to Dance

Fear is a part and parcel of performing, whether you are on the dance floor or doing something new in business. Frankly, most perfectionism comes from a fear of failure. It's not uncommon to have butterflies in your stomach before you take the stage, no matter how good you are. Barbra Streisand had a full-blown panic attack in 1967 before she went on stage in Central Park and forgot a few lyrics. Because of that she stopped performing live for 27 years. Don't let that happen to you.

Taking risks is part of being alive. It is a natural stepping-stone to a more rewarding existence. When most successful dancers are asked how they improve, they say their secret is to take calculated risks along the way. They possess a high tolerance for loss, setback, and failure and know that taking risks and learning from them is the only way to enhance their performance. They all admit to making hundreds of mistakes and errors. Risk taking in daily living can be fulfilling and rewarding. Yes, it does raise fears, yet with proper training and planning you can control your anxiety and increase the probability of a positive outcome.

Embracing risk contributes to a life of depth and breadth. Know that a full, enjoyable life, one where you push the limits of your creative, emotional, spiritual, and personal potential, will necessarily include thousands of risks and many setbacks. The pain of taking a risk must be weighed against the pain of not taking the risk, which could be a life of deep regret or remorse. There are hidden opportunities in taking big risks.

A tip for dealing with fear of risk: when you take the time to choose realistic, short-term, challenging goals, you minimize the risk factors. When you select a direction of personal passion, you fortify your courage to take the risk.

What will happen if you take a risk and experience a setback? What kind of impact will it have on your life in 3-5 years? In most cases, you'll see that the setback is meaningless aside from the wonderful lessons it can teach. This helps put it into perspective.

During the finals of a professional dance competition, each couple dances four or five times. The winner is the couple with the most first-place finishes.

So you can win a competition with only two or three first-place finishes; you could come in dead last on the other two or three dances and still win. The same thing is true in business, except one first place finish can make up for every failure you've ever had.

If you do fail, take three Cha Cha Cha steps back, and embrace the failure. The lessons you learn from your failure may change the direction of your dance. Don't fight it; see failure as a natural experience that must occur. Knowing how to handle it helps you bolster your courage to take risks. You learn that you can overcome the feelings that failure brings if your risk is unsuccessful.

Success is already yours for having the courage to take the risk at all. After all, the most damage or pain could very well come from not taking the risk to improve your business. Ask yourself, "Will this risk put me in a better position for major breakthroughs and growth?" As the English essayist Francis Bacon once said, "There is no comparison between that which is lost by not succeeding and that which is lost by not trying."

Practice Failing

The best way to prepare for mistakes is to practice them. "You can always tell how much experience a dancer has," says Genya, "by the way they recover from their mistakes. A professional will never show it. And people with less experience, they're going to make a big deal about it."

Failure is part of being human. Donny Osmond told CBS News that the only way he could get over severe stage fright was to expect something to go wrong with every performance. This made it easier to be okay about it. "I know when I walk out there, I'm not going to give the best performance," he said. "I'll make a mistake. I'll trip. I'll do something stupid. But it's OK; you pick up and just move on."[1]

Someone once said that you can only do on the competition floor what you're trained to do. So when you're training for competition, train to push past your mistakes without stopping. You will then learn how to recover from your most likely mishaps.

---

1. CBS News. (2009, February 11). *Donny Osmond confronts panic.* Retrieved from www.cbsnews.com/8301-18559_162-164444.html

Practice under the worst conditions. Use the fastest music you can. Work on a bad floor. If you can do it on a bad floor with fast music, you will likely survive anything that could happen to you in your competition; you will have trained not to let it show when there was a mistake.

Sometimes when you do something off, it feels like it lasts for half an hour – as if you continued making that one error all the way through the entire ballroom. Then you look at the video and you don't even notice because you've practiced so many times at not showing that you've made a mistake.

It helps to know what to do in difficult circumstances. Genya says he has different tricks. "If the floor is slippery, you put castor oil on the shoes. If it's cold, you get out of the room and warm up. You need to bring yourself to the right condition for dance no matter what."

As much as every dancer wants to be perfect, judges don't expect that. When Dasha is judging a competition, she wants to see "dancers expressing the best thinking condition possible, not thinking about any negative thing that happened yesterday or is happening now, or can happen." She looks for someone who is confident in their performance. "Judges see everything that's happening," she continues. "Sometimes, I'm not looking for a perfect performance. We all can lose balance, we all can miss the perfection that we're trying to achieve, but when I see that performance that they are confident in . . .to be really focused on what you're doing as of this moment, it's really, really good, and we see that right away."

Beth says that what you learn about keeping your cool while you improvise on the dance floor applies to business as well. "At Rent the Runway, we've been in a situation where we had a huge shipping day, and we looked at the weather forecast that we got from UPS, and there was going to be a monster snowstorm," she says. "We never planned for a monster snowstorm. You can't get flustered, you can't get upset, and you quickly figure out how you're going to plan your way out of it. The common denominator here is to, obviously, keep your cool, stay clear-headed, and never show on your face that you're worried. Just focus and figure out what to do and move forward."

Beth says the solution to any problem starts with a deep breath and then breaking the solution down into small pieces. "You can't swallow the elephant. If you've got a really complex problem, a business issue that you're working through, it's really helpful if you think about, 'Okay, what are all the component parts? If I can't solve the whole thing, what pieces of it can I solve? What pieces can I use to compensate for other pieces that can't be solved?' One of the things that I always teach people, or I think a lot about, is how to break things down and simplify it."

Compassionate Giving

"The day of the performance a man needs to put on the right mood with his partner, such as getting the lady a rose," says Allan. "Be genuine and unique and stay true to that." Giving to your partners, peers, or employees enhances your own performance as they look for ways to reciprocate. Bring out another's best, give them praise, help them improve, to score, to uphold a position, and the same will be provided back for you. What you give, you get back.

Give without the expectation of receiving. You'll get a rewarding feeling just from knowing you made a difference in another's life. When dancing with a partner, give them room to shine. Partner dancing is not just about you, but a true partnership.

The day of performance, you see that many dancers from the same studio, dance partners, and even judges compliment and praise dancers for how they look, how well they are performing, and how excited they are for them to compete. It is an act of giving good feelings, good vibes, good energy and good emotions to other people.

Unless you go into a competitive trance, as Genya does, try to practice this generosity of spirit beforehand. You never know if some dancer will receive the boost they need to keep going because of your words. Further, behaving in a giving way feels good! It can even help you overcome some of your own personal jitters.

Allan says that even during the competition, the best way to deal with your competitors is to cheer for them from the sidelines. Use their performance as inspiration for your own. If you've performed already, just let yourself enjoy the beauty of other artists.

On the day of performance in your business, send out good vibes to your team. Make an extra effort to be complimentary and grateful for their talents. You might even bring in some food or interesting t-shirts or badges to heighten the feeling that it's a special occasion.

As to business competitors, keep an eye on them even when you're not performing. Look for things they do well and if you run into them, compliment them. This is how we evolve socially and pave the way for future generations to take action on new ideas. And from a more selfish perspective, every positive relationship you have has the potential to be a future joint venture.

Your Main Performance Goal

A competition is about being judged and graded. Judging panels are large to enable a wide variety of views and dance philosophies. You are judged the minute you walk onto the floor. Every move has to be made with respect because the judges are always watching. Audience reaction is critical because in the early stages, all the competitors are dancing at the same time, so the judges only get a few seconds with each of the couples on the floor. Audiences react to elegance and the connection the dancers have with each other.

Make People Feel Something

Now that you're prepared to take the risk of performing, and you're ready to gracefully handle any mistake that could happen, it's time to focus on the positive side of what you're trying to accomplish in your performance: making people feel something.

As the late Maya Angelou wisely said, "People will forget what you said, people will forget what you did, but people will never forget how you made them feel."

My grandfather has dementia. It is hard to see someone deteriorate with time. Answering the same questions over and over can be very frustrating. But at the same time it bonds me with him as we try together to make the necessary adjustments. My interest in the neuroscience and psychology of things makes me more patient than most. I've learned that if new repeatable actions become part of his muscle memory, he'll perform these actions repeatedly.

One major thing that I have noticed is that he is aware of compassionate love and attention he receives from some family members, but he also remembers who feels embarrassed by him. He remembers the way they make him feel.

The easiest way to make people feel positive about you is to focus on what's important to them, not you. In dance, your audience includes the judges as well as the spectators. So when dancers compete, they have to give both of these groups a clear message. One message the judges and some of the more sophisticated members of the audience want to receive is the beauty of your technique – your turns, your posture, how grounded your body is, and the splendor of your lifts. On another level, and perhaps more important, is how you convey the message of your story. You want the people watching to feel something.

Getting people to feel comes from the acting side of dance. You can't just act "at" people. You have to internally **feel** the dance. If there is a storyline, you have to experience what your character is feeling. If your dance has no plotline, feel whatever emotion the dance itself expresses, whether that is joy, passion, or intensity.

Don't just act on the outside, indicating happiness with a smile and sadness with a frown. This will not move anyone. You have to give yourself over to the direct emotional experience and actually feel what it is you are dancing. This will inspire your audience to feel what you are feeling.

Neuroscience provides a reason for this response from your audience. Scientists have recently discovered that the brain contains mirror neurons, a type of cell that gives you the same feeling from watching someone experience something as you would if you were experiencing it yourself. That's why when you see someone else hit their funny bone, you may be the one who says, "Ow," even though nothing actually happened to you.

It's clear that when we watch other people feel something deeply, we connect to that same feeling ourselves. Bring deep feelings to your dance, and other people's minds will start to dance and be moved by what you are doing or what you are performing.

In the business world, one of the many ways you "perform" your presentation or reporting of a result is the story you give to whoever's above you in the chain of command. That could be leadership reporting to their board of directors, managers reporting to a senior executive, or employees reporting to their manager. You also present the story to people outside your company that you want to do business with. What you deliver, just like in dance, must be what THEY want. Even though you should be confident, polished, and enjoy the process of presenting, always remember it's not about showing off who you are. Your performance is about satisfying them.

For potential clients, your message should be all about how what you're offering will make their business better.

For leadership executives, your message must be:

- **Easy to understand** – Your listeners or readers have to really get what it is you're talking about, otherwise all your work was a waste of time.

- **Transferable** – Whoever you're reporting your data to must be able to easily communicate what you're talking about to others in their organization.

- **Actionable** – The information you're sharing should lead to some other action or decision within the company.

The latter applies to both inside and outside your company. When you perform, other people should want to take action based on the storyline (data or information) you're giving. Whether you want them to buy something, to inspire them, rate your performance, or to vote, what you say or write should create a result.

Marketing is another area where conveying your story and getting people to feel something is important. There's an old sales axiom that people buy emotionally and justify their purchase decision with logic.

That's part of why Apple hired likeable Zooey Deschanel from television's *New Girl* to star in a commercial about how Siri worked, back when the erstwhile telephone servant was introduced with the iPhone 4s. Deschanel is fun and easy to identify with as she asks Siri about rain, getting tomato soup delivered, and to create an appointment to clean up her apartment.

Starbucks emphasized emotion in a 2014 campaign called "Meet Me at Starbucks," which was about how people go to Starbucks to spend quality time with each other. Coffee and food were only shown to enhance emotions; a heart was in the foam of a cup of java and birthday cupcakes were presented with sparklers in them. They focused on a child playing the violin, someone break dancing, and lots of people hugging. The following taglines presented in writing across the images also added to the emotional impact: Meet me to get inspired; meet me for a good laugh; meet me I have something to share; meet me for a little surprise; every day, good things happen when we get together.

Any benefit your product offers to your customers has an emotional outcome. Pay attention to how your products give pleasure to people or help them avoid pain. That's where you can find the emotion. For example, good accountants help you get the pleasure of paying less on your taxes and using that money for something else that will bring you even more happiness, like a vacation. Pleasure is the emotion of joy. Accountants also know what to do to help you avoid audits, and they will protect you if you ever do get audited. That's avoiding pain, which gives customers a feeling of safety.

There's always something emotional you can find, no matter what your product or message. Use the emotional benefits your products offer in your storytelling and you will forge a more memorable and meaningful connection with your customers, partners, and employees.

Assertiveness

When you are performing, whether it's in dance or business, there is a sea full of competitors sharing the same space with you.

Some people develop an attitude of aggressiveness when they are competing with others for the same prize. Aggression aims to dominate an opponent. It includes a sense of ruthlessness, cruelty, or absence of compassion towards competitors. This negative, external orientation focuses energy outward onto the opponent rather than concentrating on your own performance. It generates extreme tension, fatigue, and distraction; it ultimately hinders you. When you are a spectator at a dance competition, you can easily point out performers who are too aggressive.

As a business person, you might have been told that aggressiveness is essential to success. For example, Larry Ellison, former CEO and now executive chairman and CTO of Oracle, is known for his aggressive, brash personality. But such dominating behavior alienates others by creating negative environments in which everyone is merely in it for themselves, rather than that of the greater good. Resentment and harsh feelings develop among those treated in this way, and anxiety and stress increase. Many would say that Ellison didn't care about the impact his behavior would have on others since he was already a successful billionaire. What does he have to lose? The same could be said about Steve Jobs' attitude, whose focus was on impacting society without regard for his employees. However, if you are looking to create a "worker-centered" environment where you can achieve your objectives more effectively, with greater cooperation and respect, then you need to have a different type of behavior, more like that of Sir Richard Branson, or Marc Benioff, founder and CEO of Salesforce.

The behavior that Branson and Benioff typify is that of *assertion*. Assertion is a positive behavior that emphasizes self-confidence and determination with persistence. Because you do not seek your opponent's annihilation, you can achieve success and avoid counter-reactions.

Assertiveness is not an attack technique; it will not feed an opponent's negative behavior or energy and is not destructive. It is a more powerful choice because it enables you to achieve the original objective of your aggression, which is your influence over the process and an excellent performance. Your inner strength is demonstrated in your refusal to attack your opponents' advantages or assail their integrity.

Assertiveness exhibits determination with a positive intent. It can be employed with greater consistency than aggressiveness; it is subtler and therefore more effective, shaping outcomes in a constructive way. In dance, you achieve greater levels of performance when you assert yourself and your power. Acting aggressively suggests to a competing opponent that you are insecure and uncertain about your abilities. During political debates, candidates with aggressive behavior do not project authentic confidence, whereas assertive candidates do. Even if aggression brings you short-term success, it could fail in the long run by provoking your competition in the future. Aggressive movements towards one's goal ultimately have no lasting effect.

Observe the behavior of some executives. Some present aggressive behavior, saying things in a stern tone such as, "Never take it upon yourself to _____ without my permission!" Others approach you and make a comment like, "Let's talk about _____ . Can you help explain why _____ was decided on?" The latter is assertive behavior.

When you're assertive, you improve your chances of shaping the course of events in the future. When you're aggressive you may gain power and influence for the short-term; in the long run, however, people will lose their respect for you because of your behavior and you will find that your power wanes.

Rather than be aggressive, assert yourself by using your charisma.

According to Nick Morgan, founder of Public Words, a communications consulting firm, charisma comes from focusing on a strong emotion. Put all your energy into one particular feeling, and it will communicate itself from the top of your head to the tips of your toes. "[T]he people who . . . focus on one emotion find that they compel attention," he writes in *Harvard Business Review*. "We are hard-wired to notice strong emotions in others." [1]

That hard wiring comes from the mirror neurons mentioned previously. In dance, especially in the rounds where everyone is on the dance floor at the same time, strong emotion is compelling. Use that emotion as much as you can and make sure you are aiming it at your partner as well as everywhere else. That will let the audience sense the connection between you both.

In business, show your emotion through strong convictions or enthusiasm. Use Tony Robbins or Oprah or some other well-known personality as your role model. People will respond to your passion.

---

1. Harvard Business Review. (2014, September 23). *To Build Influence, Master How You Enter a Room*. Retrieved from https://hbr.org/2014/09/to-build-influence-masterhow-you-enter-a-room

After Your Performance

Phew. You did it. In dance, you get your scores. You leave the floor. You may be happy, okay, or disappointed with how you danced, as well as the results the judges gave you. It's time to get ready for the after party!

If you're disappointed about your results, just for tonight, let it go. Don't beat yourself up or think about a million shoulda-woulda-couldas. You're human. The judges are human. Your partner is human. Everyone was doing their best, and if anyone made a mistake, that's just part of being a homo sapiens.

Save all your criticism – especially your self-criticism – for when you watch the video. On second thought, just forget about self-criticism altogether. When you watch the video, just use it as an opportunity to learn what you want to improve. We'll talk about that more in Chapter 6.

Whether you're dancing or in business, your inner critic may be so well-developed that you have a hard time silencing it. What makes us say bad things about ourselves? There is a fear of disappointing ourselves and others, and we use that to stop trying new things. That negative voice we're hearing is all in our head. If we stop being concerned about whether someone else is going to judge us, we can expand our vision and take action on our desires.

Here are some ways to quiet your inner critic:

1. Every time you think something negative about yourself or your performance – think of three positive things about yourself. For example, if you think you messed up one of your turns, think about how you showed your passion the minute you walked on the dance floor, how you shaped your frame in the Paso Doble, and how you rocked your dress and jewelry. If your inner critic is more general, saying things like, "I'm awful at everything I do," or "I'm stupid and uncoordinated," pull from a wider range of activities to support the truth of how awesome you are.

2. Write down your negative thoughts and feelings on a sheet of paper – list them. Mark Waldman says, "You can actually turn off the negative emotional circuits in your brain by being mindfully observant of them. Keep the list where you can occasionally see it, but do not throw it

away. If you do, your unconscious mind will start to ruminate on all that negativity. But when it's on a sheet of paper, there is a neural 'disconnect,' as if your brain thinks your negative thoughts and feelings are on a hard drive backup safely tucked away and on hold."

3. Sometimes we believe that we have to be perfect in order to be loved. Our inner critic comes from the idea that if we criticize ourselves first, it's safer than having to deal with the criticism of others. Say this affirmation over and over to yourself: "I can be loved just the way I am."

4. Sometimes our parents or the people who raised us may have equated being perfect with receiving love. A lot of times, our inner critic is the voice of one or both of our parents and their own self-criticism, which they projected on to us. Each time you think something critical about yourself, ask whose voice it is that you are really hearing. Is it your mother, your father, or some other authority figure? If you hear an answer, imagine that you are holding a dirty sock that belongs to one of them. Then imagine handing them back their dirty sock and let yourself be free of the criticism.

Responses from Other People

A lot of people will come up to talk to you after your performance. Some will be enthusiastic and congratulatory. Others will be lightly positive or neutral. And finally, some people always seem to find ways to be critical, without regard for the fact that after a competition or showcase, performers are at their most vulnerable.

What's interesting about human psychology is that there are potential traps in all three types of audience responses. These responses apply to business as well, although most business performance doesn't take place on one particular night.

If someone compliments you with what seems to be a decent amount of sincerity or even enthusiasm, thank them and let them know it is nice of them to say so. Really accept the compliment. Don't deflect it, either by telling them that you didn't think you were that good, or dismiss it internally because you don't think they know anything about dance or the subject. Let yourself enjoy the fact that you made someone feel good with your art and that you connected emotionally with them during your performance. Though some people may not know as much about dance as you do, they know more about what they find pleasing than you ever can. Take every compliment at face value and let it sink in and feel good.

If someone says something slightly positive like, "nice job," or something neutral like, "that was interesting," don't take it as being negative. Maybe they're not good with compliments and that's the best they could do. Maybe they didn't understand your performance or couldn't relate to it. You can't expect everyone to turn cartwheels about your routine. If they're nice enough to say something slightly positive to you, be nice enough to yourself to take it as slightly positive. Also, it's a lot better than being criticized, so don't turn it into criticism. If you have trouble avoiding that, follow the advice below.

If someone gives you negative feedback, don't take it personally. File that thought away and decide at a later time whether it has validity or not. Some people are nitpickers and will find something to criticize even when there's nothing to criticize! Ignore them. No one should be giving you negative feedback right after a performance. In fact, if there is someone in your life who has a tendency to be critical, you might want to let them know that you won't entertain any "constructive criticism" until at least three days after the performance.

But if someone does give you negative feedback after your performance, the first thing to understand is that it isn't personal. As international bestseller, Don Miguel Ruiz, writes in his book *The Four Agreements*, "Don't take anything personally....Nothing other people do is because of you. It is because of themselves." Some people take pleasure in raining on your parade. They hide and assuage their low self-esteem by saying negative things to other people. And others feel like they are only useful if they can "help you" by finding something to criticize.

Some criticism, however, is useful – even though it's insensitive to give it on the night of a performance. Lewis Howes, founder and author of *The School of Greatness*, as well as a former professional athlete, told me what he does when someone responds negatively to his work: "I used to take everything personally, but that didn't serve me, nor did it give me a clear head to serve others when I was in that state of mind. Now I look at it all as feedback. Some feedback I use to get better and other feedback I listen to and have learned to let it go."

The very nature of performing in public leaves you open to the criticism of others. One way to turn a "hater" into a fan is to smile and offer thanks for their feedback. After all, on some level, it's nice that someone cares enough, for whatever reason, to pay attention.

If you happen to notice that someone's feedback might be useful, jot it down on a piece of paper or on a note app on your smartphone. Don't bother looking at it again until you review your video, where you can see for yourself if it makes sense or not.

Do ask others in positions that you trust for their valuable feedback so you can constantly improve. Earlier in my career a corporate executive had flown down from New York to evaluate the department's presentation and reporting results. He was pretty tough with every one of my peers but didn't provide me any comments at the end of my presentation in front of the group. On the way to the airport, I asked what he really thought of my presentation. He said my presentation was like an ice sculpture, it was carved and rounded, but it needed some sanding to smooth the ice. WOW! What a compliment I thought, and I was so glad I asked.

The impact of hearing his opinion on my performance more than 15 years ago was big for me, since now I always look for ways to smooth the ice. It's always valuable to re-evaluate, as there is always room for improvement. We'll talk more about that in the next chapter.

The only way to make sense out of change is to plunge into it, move with it, and join the dance.

– ALAN WATTS

It takes time to get a dance right, to create something memorable. There must be a certain amount of polish to it.

– FRED ASTAIRE

CHAPTER 6

TAKE YOUR PERFORMANCE TO THE NEXT LEVEL

Evaluate

Winston Churchill once said, "However beautiful the strategy, you should occasionally look at the results."

This is the purpose of your post-performance review. It's time to look at the results. It's always best to do this when you're fresh. This will help you prepare for your next project, for your next initiative. It's about your evolution, and that of your business, your employees, and even your partners.

After a performance in dance, there are two possible outcomes: Either you didn't place where you wanted, in which case you have to go back to the drawing board; or you've won, in which case you have moved onto a higher level of competition, and your choreography and performance will be pushed to the next level. You still have to go back to the drawing board.

How deep a review you do depends on how soon your next competition is. "Let's say that we have a competition next week and we just finished a competition yesterday," says Genya. "You do the minor changes that you think must be done according to the video from the last performance. If you have more time, then you can do bigger changes, practice more things. You can get a little bit deeper into the problem. But resting is important. So, regardless of the result of the previous competition, you need to mentally rest. You take a day or two off."

In business, you will be measuring whether or not you met your current target goals and those of your partner's. Did you succeed at achieving your transformational change, or did you somehow get stymied from attaining what you wanted?

Celebrate either way. It's more fun to celebrate after a win, but what you learn from losing is invaluable, so that's worth celebrating, too. Plus the accomplishment of going for it is worth celebrating as well.

Whether you won or lost, go over your video or your data and documents. What you achieve next depends on knowing what worked and didn't work in your effort at transformational change.

Improvement

Don't use this time to beat yourself up over mistakes or unfulfilled promise. Concentrate instead on ways to improve your performance. Rather than focus upon outcomes, rely on improving as a result of having tried. No matter how much you know or how good you are, you can always improve. Strive to become aware of your own ignorance and shortcomings.

Ask others to help you to see where you failed and how to correct it. In professional ballroom dancing, that is why coaches are important. They can help you see faults that may have led to errors, or simply areas where there was unfulfilled potential, so you can correct them. Coaches and consultants can also help you improve your business and your personal life.

You or your coach may see a new opportunity stem from something that may have started off as a mistake. Slavik says that many interesting pieces of choreography come from dance mishaps. "If it happened, you can somehow play around that mistake, and you say, 'Oh, I can make this actually special. I can develop something from it.' Or your teacher notices and advises you to use that movement in a new way."

Coaches can only help you if you remain open to their advice. It's easy to stay attached to what you've already done, especially if you succeeded. Establish an attitude of openness to new and better ways. When you think you have all the answers, you won't see other ways. See yourself as ready and willing to take in all that may help you to improve.

Above all, don't be insulted or hurt when a coach or consultant sees something a different way than you do. For some people, there's a natural tendency towards defensiveness and defending the status quo. If you initially have issues with something a coach tells you, take a deep breath and close your mouth. Your job is to listen. Then take a day or two to let their idea sink in. I have a friend who told me he always thinks his coach is wrong for the first 24 hours after he gives him advice. He often even feels insulted by that advice. The next day, however, he comes around to a feeling of gratitude and appreciation for the helpful feedback.

Always remember that there are many ways of seeing the same thing. Here's a fun way to prove this to yourself. In 1915, a Danish psychologist named Edgar Rubin introduced the Rubin's Vase. If you look at the image in Figure 6-1, what do you initially see? Do you see a vase? Or do you see a face on the left side of the vase looking towards a symmetrical face on the right side of the vase? If you focus on the white, the object is the vase and everything else is the background. If you focus on the black, what seems like the object becomes the background, and the background shifts into the object. As you alternate visual interpretations, you can see that there is more than one correct way to view the same thing.

Figure 6-1. Vase or Faces?

As you strive for improvement, it helps to keep in mind a company or a person who you deem to be giving an ideal performance at what you want to accomplish. Pay attention to what they do well that you want to emulate. For me, Yulia Zagoruychenko is a ballroom dance role model whose level of performance I aspire to. Realistically, it is unlikely that

I will ever give a single performance that equals any one of hers; she is, however, someone who helps me to gauge what is possible in dance. Each time I make an improvement and increase my level of skill, I can look at her performances and see where I can make the next jump. For example, she has amazing leg work and leg action techniques. I am constantly aware of the beauty that is possible because of her, and as a result I am constantly improving.

One word of warning: No matter how wonderful the individual or company you are using as a role model is, you don't want to copy them or to be too derivative in your approach. Use them to inspire you to be your absolute best while at the same time maintaining your individuality.

Open your mind for other ways to improve by exploring new, related concepts. For example, you might take classes in photography or social media marketing. Something like photography would enable you to create snapshots of others' performances that could help to improve your dancing skills.

The journey to continual improvement is a slow one. Significant gain takes time. Be patient and persistent, and celebrate small strides.

Adaptation

One of the purposes for your review of your video or the data from your business initiative is to make changes for the future. There are some people who are less comfortable with change than others. If you are one of those people, remember to be flexible. Adaptation to unpredictable changes is essential for optimal performance and excellence.

Adaptation is a process of making specific adjustments in your attitude, approach, and strategies when confronted by unpredictable changes before or during a performance.

By their natures, the dance sport and business activities can be predictably unpredictable. External events, ranging from venue changes and government decisions to technological advances and even the weather, can impact your plans and your results.

Adapting is knowing when to act and when to rest. The fastest way to your best performance is to approach change with a "go with the flow" attitude.

Let your mind adapt to the changed circumstances peacefully. That will help you provide your most creative response.

Resistance to change causes tension, anxiety, and stress, all of which obstruct your potential. It is not the change that causes turmoil – it is your attitude towards that change. A flexible attitude towards change lessens its impact. Refuse to give unpredictable events the power to control your reactions. Encourage change. Accept, incorporate, and embrace it.

Don't disregard change in favor of consistency. Instead, be fluid and flexible as you change your mind due to emerging circumstances. Listen, be aware, mindful, open, and accepting of alternative possibilities.

In my company, Acolyst, we have adapted and gone through several evolutionary processes to change our business model over the years. Acolyst had evolved from a software and hardware reselling business to providing professional services to the U. S. government. Then when 9/11 occurred, we had three major United States government contracts come to a halt: ones with the Army, the Postal Service, and the State Department. The economy was bad and the government had reassessed their contract priorities. For the Post Office, the issue was anthrax, which led them to cancel our contract so they could refocus funds on security.

With these outer changes, we were struggling to stay afloat. To go with the flow, we refocused our business on IT security solutions. We wound up growing as 9/11 made security a priority for everyone, especially the government. Then we diversified our services by opening a solution center that created integrated products using components from several manufacturers. It was so successful that we were featured as a centerfold in *CRN Magazine*, a technology news periodical aimed at solution providers. The article, titled "The Anatomy of a Solution Center" showed how we partnered with technology manufacturers including IBM, CA Technologies, Intel, Lenovo, Sony, Mitratech, HP, ViewSonic, and Lexmark and integrated their products to create solutions for case management, document management, legal management, data management, storage and recovery, and much more. Eventually, these featured solutions were presented to prestigious government decision makers and influencers from the Small Business Administration (SBA), the U.S. Army, Federal Aviation Administration (FAA), Department of Justice (DoJ), and more.

Ultimately, cloud computing took over and we needed to adapt our business model once again, leading to new challenges and opportunities. But no change is ever the last change. We know that we will need to be flexible, forward thinking, and adaptable as some scenarios are out of our control and the market is continuing to evolve. Our service offerings and our delivery methods have also expanded and evolved. For example, because of our success at winning federal contracts, we are showing other technology vendors how they can market their products and services to the U. S. government.

At first we did not listen to the cry for help from the technology manufacturers we work with. We kept thinking of them as our partners, not as our clients. Several vendors came to us for help and advice in procuring government contracts, so we saw the need for this in the marketplace. We listened and adapted, creating a program that uniquely helps companies do business with the federal government, which is a completely different model from how vendors normally feature and market their products through traditional channels.

As our partners and clients came to know all the twists and turns we overcame in our business, both with the government and with the private sector, they developed a desire to understand our overall mindset and approach to our work, including the engaging, enlightening, and collaborative processes; leading to the creation of transformational projects.

The 4 R's

Whether you're reviewing your dance video or your business data, there are four steps to go through that will help you achieve what you want to accomplish in the future through continual improvement. I call these "**The 4 R's.**" To ensure optimal performance in the future that is informed by your most recent performance, you need to **re-check, re-design, re-posture, and re-position.**

1. **Re-check** - The first step is to **re-check** your performance. Did you execute what you originally intended to?

You want to re-check everything. The first part of that is to assess whether you accomplished your original plan. It's important to note what was successful as well as what didn't work. Start by asking yourself, "What went well?" It's important to take note of these successes to build on them.

We tend to ignore what was successful and only look at our failings. Make an extra effort to make sure you look for the positives here. *List five things you did well that you want to repeat in the future.*

Once you observe those, then it's time to look at what didn't work. *What took place that needs to improve?* Ask yourself or your team or your coach what led to the difficulty.

A lot of times, your foundation is the problem – how you execute basic steps that are the building blocks for everything else you do. You may be reluctant to return to what seems too simple, but it can really make a difference. Genya once asked Beth, who was partnering with him, and who, as noted in an earlier chapter, is an experienced dancer – to work on the fundamentals again with him. "I remember thinking, 'Oh, my God. I'm going to be so bored,'" she says. "But when you go back to the basics and work on improving the foundation of the basics, then all the stuff you do later becomes much, much better. Sometimes, you've got to unbundle and unpack and go back to the basics because you pick up bad habits or you over-complicate things."

Sometimes, when I work with Genya and he notices my trouble executing certain basic steps or combinations, he says that I might have picked up bad habits from previous dancing. I have to rework my muscle memory to rewire my mind and my brain because some part of my foundation or technique isn't as effective as it could be.

Beth says that the same principle applies in business as well, not just in terms of habits but in terms of unconscious reactions that occur in certain situations. "You may have scar tissue from a previous boss-subordinate relationship," she explains. "We don't always have positive relationships, so you may have conditioned yourself to react to something based on this previous relationship; there's scar tissue there. That's a bad habit. That's something that you don't want to do anymore. You've really got to train your brain to recognize when it's happening."

Sometimes a past relationship, which may have been wonderful, still has a negative effect on what you're doing now, through no fault of your past boss or partner. How they taught you to respond to certain actions may simply be out of date. It may have applied seven years ago, but it's not the way business is done today.

One example of this is the field of executive recruiting, which has changed drastically with the advent of LinkedIn and the ubiquity of mobile phones. The entire approach to finding candidates for hard to fill jobs has changed as most initial contacts are through emails. Before, recruiting was primarily something that took place by phone and word of mouth. There is a whole new culturally appropriate way to write, say, and do things to potential job candidates which is significantly different than it was a mere decade ago. While the old way may be habit for some, the new way will need to be practiced until it, too, becomes habit.

In dance, you want to re-check to make sure your footwork is the way it should be. In business, you may want to re-check to make sure you have your documents or facts in place.

In addition, review your performance from the viewpoint of the earlier aspects of the cycle: transformation, insight, the strategy map, and execution. This way you can see if any correctible errors occurred earlier in the process, before the performance phase. For example, did you miss some information that would have helped you achieve your goal with more impact? That knowledge will be useful for next time; you will realize you need to ask for information on X, Y, and Z during the insight phase.

Change occurs so rapidly that old habits need to be questioned in order to obtain the results you are looking for in your performance. These days it's social media, e-commerce, and both mobile and content marketing that are relatively new. Who knows what will be coming down the pike tomorrow. You may need to check to see if your strategy map is flexible enough to allow you to transition and to transform to new ways of doing things so that your business is responsive to whatever the current environment turns out to be.

Re-checking doesn't only apply to the technical aspects of what took place. It also applies to the story you were trying to portray. Did you convey the message you intended to convey? Sometimes the work you do in rehearsal takes you away from your core intention; it becomes a distraction. Fixing your movements during rehearsal can actually cause the original vision to be lost.

An architect has an inspiring vision in her mind before she works on the prototype and builds a model of it, but when her teammates begin to implement it, they do not know what exactly the vision in the architect's head is. In addition, through the dynamic conversations and layers of discussions that are brought in, the original vision of the design might get lost.

This concept, of course, applies no matter what your business is. You need to go back and ask, "What was my first vision? What is the actual message I am trying to bring to life?"

The phenomenon of losing your original intent occurs even when you are working on a presentation or writing material by yourself. You also need to re-check your solo work.

In business, it's important to re-check your message to your employees, not just your higher-ups. It's important for them to have a clear message. It's also important for your partners, whether those partners are internal or external, and your clients. You want to make sure your clients have a clear-cut understanding of what you're putting out there.

One place I see a lot of "Lost Message Syndrome" is when I am studying other companies' promotional YouTube videos. I'm often puzzled about the message they're trying to convey. I wonder, "How are these videos supposed to draw me in as a client?" They're technically great, jazzy, hip with the newest lingo, but they just don't tell a story that makes me want to take the next action step towards doing business with them, despite the obvious time, energy, and money that was spent. You always want to re-check your story and make sure it resonates and draws the intended reaction from your audience, and thus causes the action you want to occur.

2. **Re-design** - Once you've done your re-check, it's time for a re-design. This phase starts off by looking at what you learned from your experience, but also at changes in trends and technology that have taken place in the outside world since you started your transformation process.

One example of new tech that popped up during the writing of this book is a Facebook product called Chatbots. Chatbots interacts with you over Facebook Messenger using artificial intelligence to create conversations and provide information. Airlines are already beginning to use them to interface with travelers on the day of their flights, offering flight updates and even data-rich chat bubbles that can be clicked on to download boarding passes. Amazon and Google have similar artificial platforms with Echo and Google Plus. Microsoft has come on board in the same space with a platform that provides bot-human interactivity using text, Skype, and Office 365, among others.

If your performance initiatives were related to sales or customer service, it would behoove you to look at these new technologies. You certainly would not want to ignore them as you think about your next big push.

Always look at the design you put out and pay attention to what's available in the marketplace to make it more in tune with current lifestyles. Keep all involved parties in mind, especially your end users. Always re-design for the benefit of others and what their actual needs are. Don't rely only on what you think the market needs.

When re-designing, it makes sense to start with a fresh slate. Start by **removing everything** – all existing products, processes, positions, and people. Start with a blank plan and a clean piece of paper. Re-define the business and/or lifestyle you want to have, the value you want to offer and the position you want to own in the marketplace. Now **start adding some of the old pieces you previously had back onto the page, one by one**, intentionally and with purpose, placed into the right positions. You'll discover that not everything will make it back into the plan. You'll also notice people, products, or processes you may have taken for granted, when utilized properly, can actually create the strength and balance you need. These overlooked items might end up being the showpieces of your new business strategy plan.

You'll realize you can completely make over your business or life using **mostly your existing resources** and you will be able to see the one or two missing components needed to complete the magic equation.

In dance, re-design means looking at the choreography, the music, the costumes, the makeup, and even the story. One simple place to start is with your mistakes.

There are several factors that affect your dance in terms of the outside world. Sometimes you begin to notice trends in people's preferences. Some dancers I've spoken with have mentioned that audiences and some judges are now looking for speed and the number of spins, where in the past they were more concerned with foundation issues.

Everything evolves – even classic dances like the Rumba and the Cha Cha Cha. Rumba music has changed over time and so have the necessary leg and arm positions. That led to the dancers evolving and developing a new style, which led to more dancers competing in the Rumba than ever before. If you notice an evolution in your business, communicate with the people who are the equivalent to judges and coaches in your business to find out what the latest thinking is.

There are also trends in the outside world that you can take advantage of. The books and the movies of *Fifty Shades of Grey* were a huge part of the popular zeitgeist. You can get a lot of attention if you connect to something like that artfully. An amazing couple did a fantastic job using the songs from the movie as the score to their dance, which included the storyline, costumes, and movements similar to the movie. The female dancer, Kathrin Menzinger, starts out wearing a blindfold which, halfway through the dance, she takes off to great dramatic effect. There was even a well-timed theatrical smack performed by her partner, Vadim Garbuzov; like all theatrical "violence," its impact was greatly aided by a percussive sound effect in the music.

You may hear an extremely popular new song and think, "That song has the same rhythm and flow as the one we're dancing to." It can be advantageous to switch to something popular and be the first dancers to use a huge hit. Maurizio Vescovo and Andra Vaidilaite increased the impacts of their work by being the first professional dance champions to use Adele's Grammy won song of the year "Hello."

There are always new technologies and costume innovations that will set you apart from the other dancers, or simply make you look better. Make sure you're using the latest and greatest. Always be aware of what's available because, human nature being what it is, how you look affects how people judge your dancing and your performance.

In business, you might need to re-design your partner and client recruitment process, engagement and maintenance strategy, your pricing model or simply your website. Re-design your image to fit with the direction of the future, not the past.

3. **Re-posturing** - Your posture is how you stand and present yourself. To re-posture is to take a new stance inside yourself – a stronger stance, one that reflects the most up-to-date you, which includes your latest transformation and also the latest developments in the world around you, where you stand straighter, taller, and have more balance and control.

In business, it is about who you are overall – your posture as it is seen by the rest of the world; your brand and your voice. Part of that reflects staying aligned with your mission and what you do well from the inside out. But that will also be reflected in how you present your identity to the outside world. Re-posturing is really about the things you do to brand yourself and your business.

One place that people spend time on re-posturing is their website. Websites age. You have to stay current and make sure your website looks up to date; even company logos can begin to look clunky and dated, which is part of re-design, but also your messaging and branding needs to be up to date. With any step, back, forward, or sideways, you have learned new things that can be applied to the posture of who you are today. Your messaging needs to change as well, to reflect who your company is now, at this point in time.

My own company's website is not the same as it was five years ago, or even months ago. It won't be the same a year or two from now. We are constantly re-posturing our storyline and messaging. Your re-design must match what your audience wants, and what you want, based on how you are re-posturing.

If you have a business where you host customers on site, as part of your re-design, you might consider re-decorating or moving to a new office, even within the same building or complex. However, sometimes your environment, doesn't portray who you have become. You might need something that reflects your new expansiveness by adding media recognition plaques on the walls or putting informational booklets in the lobby or conference room that display who you are partnered with now. There are many ways to be creative. Give things a make-over.

Re-posturing for the dance sport is similar to what you're doing in business, looking at what you want and who you are as a dancer. It's also looking at your branding as a dancer. How do you want to present yourself to the world overall? What kind of dance do you want to do?

As you answer these questions, you may make certain discoveries about yourself. You may find you'd prefer more showcases and less competition or decide to focus on a certain style of dancing or a particular theme to your costumes that sends a message about who you are. For me, it is conveying a flamenco flair even if I am doing the Rumba or Cha Cha Cha dance, simply by having a flower in my hair or a certain hand articulation movement.

Then there are the dances themselves. Do you want each partner to have his or her own brand, or do you want to both do something similar? Do you want to emphasize tricks, speed, or technique? Would you like to sneak in movements from other dance styles as frequently as you can get away with it, such as incorporating some Paso in the Samba if it makes sense and is possible?

Another item to look at is the storytelling. Would you prefer your dances to be more abstract, or would you like them to have a deep story like the kind that Tabitha and Napoleon D'umo bring to their hip-hop routines on the competition show *So You Think You Can Dance?*

You can also examine your posture in terms of how you present yourself. Do you want costumes that are just at the edge of what the guidebook allows? Or do you want classic elegance? What about your haircut and hair color? What does each represent? How are you re-posturing yourself based on the feedback you have received? Are you doing something unique and original?

All of these are a vital part of your overall messaging. Having an overarching sense of who you are makes it easy for judges and audiences to establish a connection with you.

4. **Re-positioning** - Re-positioning is about making changes to help you stand out to particular audiences. This gives you a competitive advantage. What can you change that will make you stand out in front of your competitors and shine? How can you be disruptive and more impactful? This applies to business and to dance. You automatically re-position because you're trying to attract something new, something different, some new audience, some new opportunity, or some new partner.

You could be re-positioning your message for more than one specialty, like a law firm that has multiple practice areas such as personal injury and estate planning. But many times in business there are multiple audiences that will be attracted to the same product for different reasons. You create a different message for each group you want to connect with.

For example, a Broadway show is only one product, but it has to appeal to many different audiences. According to the Broadway League, in the 2015-16 season, 63% of tickets were bought by tourists from outside the New York metropolitan region, including 18% from other countries. Local audiences, account for 37% of the Broadway audience, but the 5.5% of attendees who saw 15 or more shows that year accounted for 31% of overall ticket sales.[1]

As a Broadway producer, you might want to re-position your show's advertising so that it has more appeal to foreigners. Or you might even want to think about the content of your show. For example, if you want to appeal to foreigners who may only speak English as a second language, you might want to tell more of your show's story visually rather than in words. *The Lion King* tells its story mostly visually, and it is extremely successful with foreign audiences both here in the United States and with road productions in other countries. Ask yourself, "What is the best way to competitively re-position myself to prompt people to take action to _____?" This action can represent various activities you want people to take; learn, shop, buy, sign-up, attend, etc. – fill in your blank.

---

1. The Broadway League. (2016, November). *The Demographics of the Broadway Audience 2015-2016*. Retrieved from https://www.broadwayleague.com/research/research-reports/

For re-positioning to be effective, you must understand your different customer segments. This can be extremely valuable in terms of search engine optimization (SEO) and paid advertising on search engines. Embrace the mindset of those searching. Re-position your keywords to make sure they are the most effective. Different audiences will search for different phrases. Figure out what you can do to drive more attention from each of your segments and get a higher rate of conversion. For example, you might add the keywords of "how to make" as well as "recipe for."

In dance, you re-position because you want to attain something new. Perhaps you want to get the respect and higher scores from a particular judge and you know there are particular movements that, when performed optimally and with great technique, will gain their enthusiastic approval. Perhaps you are re-positioning for a new competition event, like Blackpool Dance Festival held in England, which is a huge deal. Since it draws such a large crowd, there is a lot of competition looking to succeed. It draws dancers from around the world and only the best performers, out of the hundreds of who perform each day, win. When people say they competed and won at Blackpool, they are viewed with additional respect. As you grow in your understanding of the Blackpool culture or other competitions like the Ohio Star Ball, you realize you're going to have to re-position to stand out.

Whatever the case, re-positioning acknowledges that one size does not fit all, and that there's an element of customization that must be recognized in order to achieve the greatest success.

Reflection

At the end of the day, true evolution comes from constant improvement – and constantly checking in with yourself about what it is you want for your business, the dance sport, and for your life. It's not something you should only save for after a performance or watching a video. Even videos shouldn't be saved just for performance. You always dance better after you see yourself, even if it's just a rehearsal.

Reflection is a process that enables you to take a time out and "check-in" with your progress as a dancer or business executive.

Practicing silent reflection or inner stillness helps you to understand yourself better: your perceptions, your impressions, and the world around you. As a result, you come to know what to do and when to do it. Your timing improves so that you minimize your risk of error, setback, and failure. Periodic reflection is a way of tuning in to your mind, body, and spirit so that you can assess your training, practice, rehearsal, and competitive performances. It helps you to see what you need to polish and what you need to change. It also helps you to observe the relationship between your employees, partners, clients, and external resources.

Start a reflection practice within a week of your performance review. In a week, more changes will have occurred. They may be little, but they are worth noticing. Determine what these business or lifestyle changes are. Take time to reflect silently for at least fifteen minutes a day. Think about your priorities in life, what is important to you, and how you would prefer to use your time each day. Write these down.

Recognize and record any powerful insights you receive. Use your intuition to reflect on what your priorities are calling out for. Is something else giving you joy or emotional pleasure? Realize what has shifted in your focus and don't pressure yourself to continue doing the same thing over and over again. The best way to prioritize and find work/lifestyle balance is to delineate tasks and desires through the use of a special list. On the left side, list your "to-dos" that need your attention to maintain. Call this column "efficiency." On the right side, list unrealized goals or activities that you want or need to do and call that side "effectiveness." Spend equal time on those two lists to create a conscious balance in your work and life. This will reduce anxiety and stress if done right.

This reflection and realization teaches you that performance is the result of your priorities, not your abilities.

Your performances will have their ups and downs, subject as they are to the natural cycles of life. These reflections are necessary to become more astute in understanding the natural patterns of your performance. By aligning yourself with these rhythms, you gain power over your performance. If you are in a low period, consciously accept it and you will stop fighting it. Your performance might just improve since you are exerting less energy from trying to fight. Reflection can lead to positive growth and change.

Allan Tornsberg along with Vibeke Toft, his dance partner, say that "to achieve a goal you need to change the approach." After Allan and Vibeke did some self-reflection they shared their inner most thoughts with each other. Winning was no longer a priority, the journey of the dance was. It turned out that Vibeke loved to practice dance routines but didn't enjoy the performances as much, while Allan loved to perform but didn't enjoy all the practicing. They agreed that neither of them enjoyed competing anymore. Their priorities shifted. So they changed their focus to coaching and performing in more showcases rather than competing.

Reflection takes time and practice. As with any skill or habit, you get better the more you work at it. Work at understanding the deep relationship between your business and your personal life. Remember to reflect on all aspects including your health, your relations, and how things are going with regard to love and your financial situation. The interactions between these items contribute directly to your performance fluctuations.

Reflection helps you get a grip on reality. You are no longer discouraged when realizing that events in life can be responsible for poor performance.

The Business Mind is the Same as the Rest of Your Mind

Ultimately, there is no separate "Business Mind" that you can just plug into or switch on when you need it. We only have one mind and must make it work for everything we aim to accomplish. Visit all of your life when you reflect, with all of your mind.

The truth is, your whole mind likes to dance, not just your "Business Mind." And by dance, I mean transform and be in motion.

You can apply the same steps you've used throughout this book to any area of your life, including transforming areas that need a little magic, again and again. Start by deciding what you want to transform, get insight into where you are and what resources you already have, create a strategy map, execute on a small scale, do the full performance, then review.

Voila! Another transformation will be accomplished.

Transformation makes life exciting. Transformation brings greater fulfillment. That is the dance we are all meant to perform. For some of us it's a slow dance. For others it's a Quickstep or a Cha Cha Cha.

Once you start infusing transformation into one area of your life, it's easier to do in other areas. This also applies to your first business transformation. Your initial attempt will be the hardest, with it becoming simpler to implement additional ones in the future. What you have to do is take action. Now. A lot of people read business books and enjoy them and never make the changes that they wanted to make while they were reading. Don't be one of them. Use this book as a reference guide for the different stages of your transformation and refer back to it as you go through the process.

This book is your ticket for entrance into a transformational ballroom, whisking you from another mediocre Monday morning at the office to an exciting one in which anything is possible. Look in the mirror. Do you see that good-looking "Business Mind" checking you out?

ASK IT TO DANCE!!!

ABOUT THE AUTHOR

Valeh Nazemoff, author of international bestseller, *The Four Intelligences of the Business Mind*, is the executive vice president and co-owner of Acolyst, a data management strategy and business performance consulting services company. She is currently consulting for The White House, Executive Office of the President of the United States (EOPOTUS). Professionally known as a go-to business transformational and data strategist who has been called the "tipping point," she has led and guided project teams for many government clients, including the United States Postal Services(USPS), Social Security Administration (SSA), and Pension Benefit Guaranty Corporation (PBGC). Some of her prior customers have included Humana Healthcare, JP Morgan, FedEx, Toyota, and Yum! Brands. She has been featured on New York's Times Square and in many prestigious media publications such as *Fast Company, Thomson Reuters, Wiley, SUCCESS, Entrepreneur, Fox News, Yahoo,* and *Inc. Magazine*. Arianna Huffington herself chose to feature Valeh's voice on *The Huffington Post*, where she is now officially a Huffington Post blogger around the topics of mindful awareness and communication. Valeh is also a regular contributor to *CIO.com* through her blog series "The Mindful CIO." She is recognized as a strategic advisor, executive consultant, team builder, speaker, author, and teacher.

Her niche is transforming organizations by sharing a proven framework based on her four transformational intelligences approach where she blends research from the fields of neuroscience, psychology, organizational behavior, and analytics. Her company's methodology helps leaders and decision makers create a strategic plan and approach future challenges practically, positively, and proactively. Focusing on overall business performance, her work involves the collaboration, communication, and engagement of various organizational departments including marketing, IT, legal, finance, HR, and operations. Valeh enjoys problem solving and loves taking the puzzle pieces of a distressed organization then helping to create order from chaos. She is known as a firefighter who brings her energy and intention to helping businesses get back on track from their delayed projects.

She has consulted for clients of CA Technologies, been engaged by Lockheed Martin and CACI International, and coached and conducted workshops which included attendees from Harvard University, IBM, Walmart, and Erie Insurance. She has taught and mentored students from George Mason University, the University of Mary Washington, the University of Phoenix, and Marymount University on various business topics and skills. Valeh has a BS in psychology from George Mason University, and MBAs in e-business and global management from the University of Phoenix.

Valeh is the recipient of several leadership awards and was recognized for four consecutive years on *CRN Magazine*'s 2016, 2015, 2014 and 2013 "Women of the Channel" lists.

Valeh is also a book reviewer for the New York Journal of Books. Books are provided by the major top publishers in the world. Some of her book reviews have been of the work of authors who are influential leaders and high-status speakers like Sallie Krawcheck and Jill Konrath.

She's a competitive ballroom dancer dancing the Rumba, Cha Cha Cha, Samba, Paso Doble and now practicing the Argentine Tango. She is based in the Washington, DC / Baltimore, MD metro area. She invites comments and inquiries at valeh.nazemoff@acolyst.com.

AUTHOR ENGAGEMENT

Speaking, Coaching, Consulting Related Engagements:

Valeh Nazemoff's speaking, executive coaching, seminars, half-day or full-day workshops, assessments, consulting, and other business engagements will bring life to various decision makers in your organization and get their minds dancing. Valeh will inspire your group with her passion and engaging style. You'll be entertained, motivated, and educated. She can customize a program just for your needs. If you are interested in learning more about her programs and services, contact Valeh at valeh.nazemoff@acolyst.com.

You can also connect with Valeh here:

Twitter: https://twitter.com/valehnazemoff

Facebook: https://www.facebook.com/OfficialValehNazemoff/

About Acolyst's Project Related Engagements:

Valeh is executive vice president and co-owner of Acolyst, which helps businesses harness the ever-increasing volume of data being received daily and use it to make proactive, strategic decisions. The workplace has gotten more complicated over the years with the overload of data and decision making, and both the government and commercial sectors need Acolyst's transformational help more than ever. Using an innovative blend of neuroscience, organizational psychology, and analytics, Acolyst delivers data management strategy and business performance consulting services that achieve measurable and sustainable results. Acolyst is proud to provide exceptional data management, business performance, governance, records, case (GRC), & legal matter management consulting services including documentation and technology solutions.

If you get all tangled up, just tango on.

– AL PACINO IN SCENT OF A WOMAN

Fly high, feel the music, and forever dance free.

– PHOENIX Z COURTNEY

*Sometimes we focus on the lyrics too much
and forget to dance to the music.*

– ALEXA ANDERSON

Made in the USA
San Bernardino, CA
28 August 2017